# BE DELIVERED

# Be Delivered

## WARREN W. WIERSBE

While this book is intended for
the reader's personal enjoyment
and profit, it is also designed for
group study. Study questions are
located at the end of the text.

Chariot Victor Publishing
A Division of Cook Communications

Chariot Victor Publishing,
A division of Cook Communications, Colorado Springs, Colorado 80918
Cook Communications, Paris, Ontario
Kingsway Communications, Eastbourne, England

Editor: Barbara Williams
Design: Bill Gray
Cover Photo: Image Bank
Study Questions: Susan Moroney

1  2  3  4  5  6  7  8  9  10  Printing/Year  02  01  00  99  98

# CONTENTS

# PREFACE

Whether it means freeing a nation from political bondage or delivering an indivdual from dependence or codependence, liberation is a popular theme these days.

But many people who want to be free don't really know what freedom is or how to use it if they have it. "Unless a man has the talents to make something of himself, freedom is an irksome burden," wrote the longshoreman philosopher Eric Hoffer in *The True Believer*, and he is right. Fools use freedom as a toy to play with; wise people use freedom as a tool to build with.

The nation of Israel is a case in point. God brought them out of Egypt that He might bring them into their inheritance (Deut. 4:37-38), but they didn't have the maturity to manage their freedom successfully. As a result, a whole generation of Israelites perished while wandering in the wilderness.

Using the experiences of Israel as Exhibit A, the Book of Exodus explains what true freedom is, what freedom costs, and how it must be used. Exodus teaches us that freedom is not license and discipline is not bondage. God tells us how to enjoy mature freedom in His will, a quality that is desperately needed in our churches and our world today. The privilege of freedom is precious, the responsibilities of freedom are serious, and we can't have the one without the other. I trust that your personal application of the spiritual principles found in Exodus will bring you into the true freedom that Christians have in Jesus Christ.

Warren W. Wiersbe

# A Suggested Outline of the Book of Exodus

Key theme: God sets us free that we might serve Him
Key verses: Exodus 6:6-8

## I. Redemption: The Lord Delivers His People—1–18
"I will bring you out"(Ex. 6:6)
1. The Lord calls a leader—1–4
2. The Lord declares war on Pharaoh—5–10
3. The Lord wins the victory—11:1–15:21
4. The Lord provides for His people—15:22–17:16
    Healing —15:22-27
    Meat—16:1-13
    Manna—16:14-36
    Water— 17:1-7
    Protection—17:8-16
5. The Lord counsels His leader—18

## II. Covenant: The Lord Claims His People—19–24
"I will take you to Me for a people"(Ex. 6:7)
1. The people prepare—19
2. The Lord declares His law—20–23
3. The covenant confirmed by blood—24

## III. Worship: The Lord Dwells with His People—25–40
"I will be to you a God"(Ex. 6:7)
1. Instructions about the tabernacle—25–27; 30–31
2. Consecration of the priests—28–29
3. Disobedience of the people—32–34
4. Construction of the tabernacle—35–39
5. God's glory enters the tabernacle—40

Note the balance in the spiritual experience of the Jewish people: God delivered them from bondage (1–18), but freedom should lead to obedience (19–24), and obedience results in worship to the glory of God (25–40). Apart from worship, freedom becomes lawlessness and obedience becomes oppression.

# Wanted: A Deliverer

The little girl who defined "radio" as "television without pictures" didn't know what she was talking about. I grew up in the Golden Age of Radio, and I can assure you that as I listened, I saw many vivid and exciting pictures—right in my own imagination. Television doesn't let you do that. And the stories on radio went on and on, day after day, always leaving us wondering, "What will happen next?"

The Old Testament is God's "continued story" of His great program of salvation that He announced to Adam and Eve (Gen. 3:15) and to Abraham (12:1-3). That explains why the Hebrew text of Exodus begins with the word "and," for God is continuing the story He started in Genesis.[1] God's wonderful story finally led to the coming of Jesus to earth and His death on the cross, and it won't end until God's people go to heaven and see Jesus on the throne. What a story!

The theme of Exodus is *deliverance,* and you can't have deliverance without a deliverer. That's where Moses comes in, the great liberator, legislator, and mediator.

## 1. The deliverer needed (Ex. 1:1-22)

The Jewish rabbis call Exodus "the Book of Names" (or "These Are the Names") because it opens with a list of the names of the sons of Jacob (Israel) who brought their families to Egypt to escape the famine in Canaan (Gen. 46).[2] God used Israel's experiences in Egypt to prepare them for the special tasks He gave them to accomplish on earth: bearing witness to the true and living God, writing the Holy Scriptures and bringing the Savior into the world.

*Blessing (Ex. 1:1-7).* During the years Joseph served as second ruler in Egypt, his family was greatly respected; and even after Joseph died, his memory was honored in the way the Egyptians treated the Hebrews. God kept His covenant promise to Abraham by blessing his descendants and causing them to multiply greatly (Gen. 12:1-3; 15:5; 17:2, 6; 22:17). By the time of the Exodus, there were more than 600,000 men who were twenty years and older (Ex. 12:37; 38:26); and when you add the women and children, the total could well be nearly 3 million people, all of whom descended from the original family of Jacob. God certainly kept His promise!

But a new Pharaoh wasn't happy with the rapid multiplication of the Jewish people, so he took steps to control it.

*Step #1—Afflicting the adults (Ex. 1:8-14).* God had told Abraham that his descendants would go to a strange country and there be enslaved and mistreated, but He had promised that He would set them free by His power at the right time (Gen. 15:12-14). God compared Egypt to a smoking furnace (v. 17; see Deut. 4:20) where His people would suffer, but their experience in that furnace would transform the Israelites into a mighty nation (Gen. 46:3).

During the centuries the Jews had been in Egypt (15:13; Ex. 12:40-41), they had seen many Egyptian dynasties come and go; but who was the new king who was ignorant of Joseph and his family and tried to destroy "the people of the children of Israel"?[3] The 17th Dynasty, the Hyksos,[4] were foreigners and "strangers" in the land as were the Jews, so they were probably sympathetic with Israel; but the 18th Dynasty was Egyptian and their rulers expelled foreigners from the land. This may have been the dynasty that began the persecution of the people of Israel.

Why would the Egyptians want to make life miserable for the Jews? Israel was a source of blessing in the land, as Joseph had been before them (Gen. 39:1-6), and they weren't causing trouble. Pharaoh's stated reason was that the presence of so many Jews was a security risk: since the Jews were outsiders, if there were an invasion, they would no doubt ally themselves with the enemy. However, whether Pharaoh realized it or not, the real cause was the conflict announced in 3:15, the enmity between the people of God and the children of Satan, a conflict that still goes on in the world today.

No people in recorded history have suffered as the Hebrew people have suffered, but every nation or ruler that has persecuted the Jews has been punished for it. After all, God's promise to Abraham was, "I will bless those who bless you, and I will curse him who curses you" (12:3, NKJV). God kept that promise in the way He dealt with Egypt and Babylon in ancient days and Stalin and Hitler in modern times. God is long-suffering as He sees nations persecute His chosen people, but eventually His hand of judgment falls on the oppressors.

The Egyptian taskmasters "worked them ruthlessly" (Ex. 1:13, NIV), forcing the Jewish slaves to build cities and work in the fields. But the blessing of God caused the Israelites to continue to multiply, and this frightened and enraged their captors even more. Something else had to be done to keep Israel under control.

*Step #2—Killing the Jewish boys at birth (Ex. 1:15-21)*. If

11

this plan had succeeded, Pharaoh would have wiped out the Hebrew people. The future generation of men would be dead and the girls would eventually be married to Egyptian slaves and absorbed into the Egyptian race. But Genesis 3:15 and 12:1-3 said that God would not permit such a thing to happen, and He used two Jewish midwives to outwit Pharaoh.[5]

This is the first instance in Scripture of what today we call "civil disobedience," refusing to obey an evil law because of a higher good. Scriptures like Matthew 20:21-25; Romans 13; and 1 Peter 2:11 admonish Christians to obey human authorities; but Romans 13:5 reminds us that our obedience must not violate our conscience. When the laws of God are contrary to the laws of man, then "[w]e ought to obey God rather than men" (Acts 5:29). You see this exemplified not only in the midwives but also in Daniel and his friends (Dan. 1; 3; 6) and the apostles (Acts 4–5).[6]

Were the midwives lying to Pharaoh? Probably not.[7] The babies were born before the midwives arrived because Shiphrah and Puah had told their assistants to be late! God blessed the two leading midwives for putting their own lives on the line in order to save the Jewish nation from extinction. However, He honored these two women in a strange way: He gave them children at a time when it was dangerous to have children! Perhaps all their children were daughters, or perhaps God protected their sons as He protected Moses. However, this blessing from God shows how precious children are to the Lord: He wanted to give these two women His very best reward, so He sent them children (Ps. 127:3).

*Step #3—Drowning the male babies (Ex. 1:22).* When Pharaoh discovered he'd been deceived, he changed his plan and commanded all his people to see to it that the Jewish male babies were drowned in the sacred Nile River. Pharaoh's police couldn't check up on every Jewish midwife, but the Egyptian people could keep their eyes on the Jewish slaves and report when a boy was born. But one boy would be born that Pharaoh couldn't kill.

## 2. The deliverer born (Ex. 2:1-10)[8]

Amram and Jochebed were Moses' parents (6:20), and while the Exodus text emphasizes the faith of the mother, Hebrews 11:23 commends both the father and the mother for trusting God. Certainly it took faith for them to have normal marital relations during that dangerous time when Jewish babies were being killed. Moses became a great man of faith, and he learned it first from his godly parents. Amram and Jochebed already had two children: Miriam, who was the oldest, and Aaron, who was three years older than Moses (Ex. 7:7).

From the very first, Moses was seen to be "no ordinary child" (Acts 7:20, NIV; see Heb. 11:23),[9] and it was evident that God had a special purpose for him. Believing this to be true, the parents defied Pharaoh's edict and kept their son alive. This wasn't easy to do since all the Egyptians were now Pharaoh's official spies, watching for babies to be drowned (Ex. 1:22).

Jochebed obeyed the letter of the law when she put Moses in the waters of the Nile, but certainly she was defying Pharaoh's orders in the way she did it. She was trusting the providence of God and God didn't fail her. When the princess came to the Nile to perform her religious ablutions, she saw the basket, discovered the baby, and heard him cry; and her maternal instincts told her to rescue the child and care for him.

God used a baby's tears to control the heart of a powerful princess, and He used Miriam's words to arrange for the baby's mother to raise the boy and get paid for it! The phrase "as weak as a baby" doesn't apply in the kingdom of

BE DELIVERED

God; for when the Lord wants to accomplish a mighty work, He often starts by sending a baby. This was true when He sent Isaac, Joseph, Samuel, John the Baptist, and especially Jesus. God can use the weakest things to defeat the mightiest enemies (1 Cor. 1:25-29). A baby's tears were God's first weapons in His war against Egypt.

The princess adopted Moses as her own son, which means that Moses had a favored position in the land and was given a special education for service in the government (Acts 7:22). In the Egyptian language, Moses means "born" or "son" and sounds like a Hebrew word that means "to draw out" (of the water). Years later, his name would remind Moses of the God who rescued him and did great things for him in Egypt. On more than one occasion, Moses would rescue his people because he trusted the Lord.

**3. The deliverer prepared (Ex. 2:11-25)**
Moses spent his first forty years (Acts 7:23) serving in the Egyptian bureaucracy. (Some students think he was being groomed to be the next pharaoh.) Egypt seems the least likely place for God to start training a leader, but God's ways are not our ways. In equipping Moses for service, God took several approaches.

*Education.* "And Moses was learned in all the wisdom of the Egyptians, and was mighty in words and deeds" (Acts 7:22, NKJV). What did that involve? Egypt had a highly developed civilization for its time, particularly in the areas of engineering, mathematics, and astronomy. Thanks to their knowledge of astronomy, they developed an amazingly accurate calendar, and their engineers planned and supervised the construction of edifices that are still standing. Their priests and doctors were masters of the art of embalming, and their leaders were skilled in organization and administration. Visitors to Egypt today can't help but be impressed with the accomplishments of this ancient people. The servant of God should learn all he can, dedicate it to God, and faithfully serve God.

*Failure (Ex. 2:11-14)*. Though some people were confused about his racial identity (v. 19), Moses knew that he was a Hebrew and not an Egyptian, and he couldn't help but identify with the plight of his suffering people. One day he made a courageous decision to help his people, even if it meant losing his noble position as the adopted son of the royal princess (Heb. 11:24-26). The pleasures[10] and treasures of Egypt faded from view as he saw himself helping to liberate God's chosen people.

It's possible that the Egyptian officer wasn't just disciplining the Jewish slave but was beating him to death, because the Hebrew word can mean that, so when Moses interfered, he was probably saving a man's life. And, if the Egyptian officer turned on Moses, which is likely, then Moses was also defending his own life.

But if Moses was planning to free the Hebrews by killing the Egyptians one by one, he was in for a shock. The next day he discovered that the Egyptians were only part of the problem *because the Jews couldn't even get along with each other!* When he tried to reconcile the two Jews, they rejected his help! Even more, he learned that his secret was out and that Pharaoh was after his life. There was only one thing to do and that was to flee.

These two incidents reveal Moses as a compassionate man who was sincere in his motives but impetuous in his actions. Knowing this, you would never suspect that later he would be called "the meekest man on the earth" (Num. 12:3). Moses' failure to help free the Jews must have devastated him. That's why God took him to Midian and made him a shepherd for forty years. He had to learn that deliverance would come from God's hand, not Moses' hand (Acts 7:25;

Ex. 13:3).

*Solitude and humble service (Ex. 2:15-25)*. Moses became a fugitive and fled to the land of the Midianites, relatives of the Jews (Gen. 25:2). True to his courageous nature, he assisted the daughters of Reuel, the priest of Midian (Ex. 2:18), and this led to hospitality in their home and marriage with one of the daughters, Zipporah, who bore him a son.[11] Later, she would bear another son, Eliezer (18:1-4; 1 Chron. 23:15). Reuel ("friend of God") was also known as Jethro (Ex. 3:1; 18:12, 27), but Jethro ("excellence") may have been his title as priest rather than his given name.[12]

The man who was "mighty in word and deed" is now in the lonely pastures taking care of stubborn sheep, but that was just the kind of preparation he needed for leading a nation of stubborn people. Israel was God's special flock (Ps. 100:3) and Moses His chosen shepherd. Like Joseph's thirteen years as a slave in Egypt and Paul's three years' hiatus after his conversion (Gal. 1:16-17), Moses' forty years of waiting and working prepared him for a lifetime of faithful ministry. God doesn't lay hands suddenly on His servants but takes time to equip them for their work.

God's delays aren't evidence of unconcern, for He hears our groans, sees our plight, feels our sorrows, and remembers His covenant. What He has promised, He will perform, for He never breaks His covenant with His people. When the right time comes, God immediately goes to work.

### 4. The deliverer called (Ex. 3:1–4:17)

Moses spent forty years serving as a shepherd in Midian (Acts 7:23; Ex. 7:7), and during those many days and nights in the field, he no doubt meditated on the things of God and prayed for his people who were suffering in Egypt. It's significant that God calls people who are busy: Gideon was threshing grain (Jud. 6), Samuel was serving in the tabernacle

(1 Sam. 3), David was caring for sheep (17:20), Elisha was plowing (1 Kings 19:19-21), four of the apostles were managing their fishing business (Mark 1:16-20), and Matthew was collecting taxes (Matt. 9:9). God has nothing good to say about laziness (Prov. 24:30-34; Matt. 25:26-27; 2 Thes. 3:10-12).

*What Moses saw (Ex. 3:1-4)*. God can take an insignificant bush, ignite it, and turn it into a miracle; and that's what He wanted to do with Moses. Some see in the burning bush a picture of the nation of Israel: they are God's light in the world, persecuted but not consumed. But the burning bush was also a picture of what God had planned for Moses: he was the weak bush but God was the empowering fire (19:18; 24:17; Deut. 4:24; Jud. 13:20; Heb. 12:29); and with God's help, Moses could accomplish anything.

*What Moses heard (Ex. 3:5-10)*. God spoke to Moses and assured him that He was the God of his fathers and that He felt the suffering of the Jews in Egypt. He was now ready to deliver them out of Egypt and lead them into the Promised Land, and Moses would be His chosen leader.[13] God's statement "Behold, I will send you" must have astonished Moses. Why would God choose a failure?

*What Moses did (Ex. 3:1–4:17)*. Moses should have rejoiced because God was at last answering prayer, and he should have submitted to God's will saying, "Here I am! Send me!" But instead, he argued with the Lord and tried to escape the divine call to rescue Israel from slavery. In Egypt, forty years before, Moses had acted like the impetuous horse and rushed ahead of God, but now he is acting like the stubborn mule and resisting God (Ps. 32:9). Moses gave five reasons why he couldn't accept God's call.

*(1) "I'm a nobody" (Ex. 3:11-12)*. What Moses thought of himself, or what others thought of Moses, really wasn't important. God had spoken and that was all Moses needed

for assurance that he was the right man for the job. Had forty years of shepherding so extinguished the fire in his soul that he didn't think he could serve the Lord? Why was he looking at himself instead of looking by faith to the Lord? "I will be with you" is all the assurance God's servants need in order to succeed (Josh. 1:5; Isa. 41:10; 43:5).

*(2) "I don't know Your name" (Ex. 3:13-22).* As the representative of God, Moses had to be able to disclose His character to the Jewish people. Of course, God's name "Jehovah" had been known centuries ago (Gen. 4:26) and was familiar to the patriarchs (14:22; 15:1; 25:21-22; 28:13; 49:18). What Moses asked was, "What does Your name mean? What kind of a God are You?" God explained that the name Jehovah is a dynamic name, based on the Hebrew verb "to be" or "to become." He is the self-existent One who always was, always is, and always will be, the faithful and dependable God who calls Himself "I AM."[14] Centuries later, Jesus would take the name "I AM" and complete it: "I am the bread of life" (John 6:35), "I am the light of the world" (8:12), "I am the true vine" (15:1), and so on.

The eternal God knows the end from the beginning, so He was able to tell Moses exactly what would happen when he returned to Egypt (Ex. 3:16-22). The elders of Israel would accept Moses as their leader and believe that God was about to deliver them. The king of Egypt would resist God's message and suffer the terrible judgments of God. The people of Israel would be delivered from the land and spoil the Egyptians and thus receive the wages they hadn't been paid during their years of slavery.

*(3) "The elders won't believe me" (Ex. 4:1-9).* "They will not believe" really means "I do not believe." Moses was concerned about his credentials before the Jewish elders, so God gave him three signs to convince the elders that he was truly God's chosen servant. "The Jews require a sign"

(1 Cor. 1:22). From now on, Moses will experience God's power and work miracles.

*(4) "I'm not a fluent speaker" (Ex. 4:10-12).* Moses completely missed the message of God's name and God's miraculous power. "I AM" is all that we need in every circumstance of life, and it's foolish for us to argue, "I am not." If God can turn rods into serpents and serpents into rods, if He can cause and cure leprosy, and if He can turn water into blood, then He can enable Moses to speak His Word with power.[15] Moses was making the mistake of looking at himself instead of looking to God (6:12). The God who made us is able to use the gifts and abilities He's given us to accomplish the tasks He assigns to us.

Was Moses manifesting an attitude of pride or true humility? Forty years before, he felt perfectly adequate to face the enemy and act on behalf of his people, but now he's backing off and professing himself to be a worthless failure. But humility isn't thinking poorly of ourselves; it's simply not thinking of ourselves at all but making God everything. The humble servant thinks only of God's will and God's glory, not his or her own inadequacy, success, or failure. Moses was clothing his pride and unbelief in a hollow confession of weakness.

*(5) "Somebody else can do it better" (Ex. 4:13-17).* "O Lord, please send someone else to do it" (v. 13, NIV). Moses calls Him "Lord" and yet refuses to obey His orders (Luke 6:46; Acts 10:14). Most of us understand that attitude because we've made the same mistake. If God isn't Lord of all, He isn't Lord at all.

In His anger, God appointed Aaron to be the spokesperson for Moses, but Aaron wasn't always a help to his brother. It was Aaron who cooperated with the people in making the golden calf (Ex. 32), and Aaron and his sister Miriam were critical of Moses and his wife and brought trouble to the

camp (Num. 12). There's the suggestion in Exodus 4:14 that
in accepting Aaron, Moses was confusing the Old Testament
ministries; for Aaron was to be the priest and Moses the
prophet. When God in His anger gives us what we selfishly
want, that gift rarely turns out to be a blessing (Num. 11:33;
Hosea 13:11). One of the most painful judgments God can
send is to let His people have their own way.

Subsequent events proved that Moses was very capable
of speaking God's words with mighty power, both to his own
people and to the king of Egypt. As the history of Israel
unfolds, you find Moses delivering some eloquent messages
in the power of the Lord. The Book of Deuteronomy records
his magnificent farewell speech.

The lesson is plain: God knows us better than we know
ourselves, so we must trust Him and obey what He tells us to
do. When we tell God our weaknesses, we aren't sharing
anything He doesn't already know (Jud. 6:15; 1 Sam. 9:21;
Jer. 1:6). The will of God will never lead you where the power
of God can't enable you, so walk by faith in His promises.

## 5. The deliverer sent (Ex. 4:18-31)

When you've lived in a place for forty years, how do you go
about packing up and moving elsewhere, especially when
you're going to a place of danger? The text describes five
encouragements God gave Moses as he sought to obey the
will of God.

*His father-in-law's blessing (Ex. 4:18).* Moses couldn't leave
without first informing his father-in-law and receiving his permission and blessing. However, there's no record that Moses
told Jethro of his meeting with Jehovah and his call to deliver
the people of Israel from bondage. All he told Jethro was that
he wanted to visit Egypt to see if his family was still alive.

*The promises of God (Ex. 4:19-23).* As Moses stepped out
by faith, God spoke to him and encouraged him. God told

Moses not to be afraid to return to Egypt because his enemies were dead. Then He assured Moses that He would enable him to do the miraculous signs but that Pharaoh would only harden his heart and thereby invite more judgments from the Lord. Before Moses even arrived in Egypt, he knew he had a battle on his hands. It wouldn't be easy to convince Pharaoh to let his Jewish slaves go free.

God also assured Moses of His special love for Israel, His firstborn son (Jer. 31:9; Hosea 11:1). In the ancient world, the firstborn in every family had special rights and privileges, and God would see to it that Israel, His firstborn, would be redeemed and rewarded, while the firstborn of Egypt would be slain. God was reminding Moses that he was the servant of a great God who knew what He would do. The key to victory was faith in the Lord.

*Zipporah's obedience (Ex. 4:24-26).* Moses had neglected to circumcise his second son, Eliezer, and God struck Moses down with an illness that could have taken his life. We get the impression that when Moses had circumcised Gershom, his firstborn, Zipporah had been appalled by the ceremony and therefore had resisted having Eliezer circumcised. Moses let her have her way and this displeased the Lord. After all, Moses couldn't lead the people of Israel if he was disobedient to one of the fundamental commandments of the Lord (Gen. 17:10-14). Even if the Jews didn't know it, God knew about his disobedience, and He was greatly displeased.

The servant of the Lord must be careful to "manage his own family well" (1 Tim. 3:4, NIV) if he expects to enjoy the blessings of the Lord; for "[i]f anyone does not know how to manage his own family, how can he take care of God's church?" (v. 5, NIV)

*Aaron's arrival (Ex. 4:27-28).* At Horeb (another name for Mt. Sinai; 19:10-11; Deut. 4:10), Moses met his elder brother Aaron who would be his companion and associate for the next forty years. When it comes to serving the Lord, two are better than one (Ecc. 4:9). Jesus sent out His disciples in pairs (Mark 6:7) and God called Paul and Barnabas together to take the Gospel to the Gentiles (Acts 13:2). In spite of his faults, and we all have a few, Aaron ministered along with Moses and became the founder of the priesthood in Israel.

*The nation's faith (Ex. 4:29-31).* Moses had expressed fear that the Jewish elders wouldn't believe his message or accept his leadership, but they did, and so did the rest of the nation when they saw the demonstration of God's power in the signs. On hearing that God was concerned for them and was about to rescue them, they bowed in grateful worship. Worship is the logical response of God's people to God's grace and goodness.

This was the lull before the storm. God was about to declare war on Egypt and Pharaoh, and life for the Jews would become more difficult before it would get better.

# T W O

# *War Is Declared*

If Moses and Aaron had been privileged to listen to Jonathan Edwards preach his famous sermon "Sinners in the Hands of an Angry God," they probably would have shouted "Amen!" when Edwards said:

> All the kings of the earth, before God, are
> as grasshoppers; they are nothing, and less than
> nothing: both their love and their hatred is to
> be despised. The wrath of the great King of kings,
> is as much more terrible than theirs, as his majesty
> is greater.[1]

Hearing those words, Moses and Aaron would have recalled the day they stood before the ruler of one of the greatest kingdoms of the ancient world.[2] They were sent by God to inform Pharaoh that if he didn't release the Jewish people, Jehovah would declare war on him and his gods and wouldn't stop attacking Egypt until the people of Israel were set free. God's two ambassadors had one message from the Lord: "Let My people go—or else!"[3] Pharaoh's responses to Moses and Aaron were predictable: he rejected God's command, disdained the miracles Moses and Aaron performed, and deliberately hardened his heart against the Lord.

## 1. Pharaoh rejects God's Word (Ex. 5:1–6:27)
Their request was a simple one: Moses and Aaron wanted per-

mission to take the Jewish people three days' journey into the desert to a place where they could worship the Lord.[4] Six days of travel and one day of worship would add up to a week away from their work, but Moses said nothing about how long they would be gone or when they would return. This omission made Pharaoh suspicious, and he wondered if the purpose of their journey was escape rather than worship. Three questions are involved in this episode.

*Pharaoh: "Why should I obey the Lord?" (Ex. 5:1-3)* This was a reasonable question because the Egyptian people considered Pharaoh to be a god, and why should their king obey a strange god that neither Pharaoh nor the Egyptians knew? Furthermore, what right did this new god have to call the Israelites "My people" when the Jews were the slaves of Pharaoh? If Pharaoh obeyed the edict, he would be acknowledging a deity greater than himself, and he wasn't about to do that. In his pride and false security, Pharaoh wouldn't listen to the words of the living God.

Moses mentioned that the Israelites might be in danger of being killed if they failed to obey the Lord. Why bring that up? Perhaps Moses was hinting that Pharaoh's stubbornness might cost him his slaves and that he'd be better off to give the Jews a week off and thereby protect his cheap labor. However, there's another factor involved: Moses was telling Pharaoh that the God of the Hebrews was a powerful God who could kill the Egyptians as well as the Jews. Pharaoh needed to understand that the demands Moses and Aaron were making were not to be taken lightly, for this was a matter of life and death.

*Pharaoh: "Why should the work stop?" (Ex. 5:4-21)* The enslavement of the Israelites was a great boost to the economy of Egypt, and Pharaoh wasn't about to give up a good thing. As dictators have done for centuries, Pharaoh exploited a captive people and was unconcerned about their welfare.

Unknown to the king, God was working out His perfect plan to free His people and glorify His great name; and nothing Pharaoh could do would prevent God's plan from succeeding.

Instead of giving the Jews relief from their toil, Pharaoh made their labor even harder. He refused to give them the straw they needed for the manufacturing of the clay bricks, but he demanded that they still reach their assigned daily quotas. "If they have so much time on their hands that they can take a week off," he argued, "then let them find their own straw. The extra work will take their minds off such foolish ideas." God's message to Pharaoh through Moses and Aaron was only "vain words" as far as the king was concerned (v. 9; "lies," NIV).

When their work became unbearable because of the new rules, the Hebrews sent their foremen to protest to Pharaoh. It's unusual that slaves would have access to the king, but Pharaoh knew what he was doing. He told them what Moses and Aaron had demanded of him, and this turned the Jewish foremen against the leaders God had given them. The foremen told Moses and Aaron what they thought of them and then slandered them among the Jews. This wouldn't be the last time Moses would be opposed by his own people who didn't understand what the Lord was doing.

Instead of going to Pharaoh to complain, the foremen should have gone to Moses and Aaron and suggested that they summon the elders and have a prayer meeting. They should have reminded themselves of the promises God had given Israel and claimed them by faith. What a difference that would have made for them and for their leaders! Alas, during the next forty years, complaining about God's will and criticizing God's leaders would be characteristic of the people of Israel; but are God's people much different today?

*Moses: "Why have You sent me?" (Ex. 5:22–6:27)* Moses did what all spiritual leaders must do when the going is tough: he

25

took his burden to the Lord and honestly talked to Him about the situation. It's easy to see that Moses was disappointed and distressed. He blamed God for the way Pharaoh was mistreating the Jews, and he accused Him of doing nothing. "Is this why You sent me?" he asked (5:22, NIV). In other words, "Are You going to keep Your promises to me or not?"

God's chosen servants must expect opposition and misunderstanding, because that's part of what it means to be a leader; and leaders must know how to get alone with God, pour out their hearts, and seek His strength and wisdom. Spiritual leaders must be bold before people but broken before God (see Jer. 1) and must claim God's promises and do His will even when everything seems to be against them.

How did the Lord encourage His struggling servant? To begin with, *God spoke to him and gave him great promises (Ex. 6:1-8).* Today we have the written Word of God, but it's likely that Moses heard God speak in an audible voice (33:11; Deut. 34:10). Four times in this speech, God reminded Moses, "I am the Lord" (Ex. 5:2, 6, 7, 8)[5] and used His covenant name "Jehovah"; and seven times, God said, "I will." When we know that God is in control and we claim His promises, then we can experience peace and courage in the battles of life. God promised to bring Israel out of Egypt, free them from bondage, and take them into their Promised Land. At the heart of the seven "I will" promises is "And I will take you to Me for a people" (v. 7), which is the basis for all that God did for the Jews.

God also reminded Moses of *His covenant name "Jehovah" (6:3).* One way to get to know God better is to pay attention to His names. The patriarchs knew God as "God Almighty,"[6] which in the Hebrew is "El Shaddai—the all-sufficient and all-powerful God," and they knew that God's name was "Jehovah" (Yahweh); but they didn't understand the full implications of the name. God had explained the name "Jehovah" to Moses when He called him in Midian (3:13-14), but now He associated His name with the covenant He would make with His people (6:4). Jehovah is the special name of God that links Him with Israel and His covenants, and it is so sacred to Jews even today that they will not speak it when they read the Scriptures in the synagogue. Instead, they substitute "Adonai" (Master) or simply say "the Name."

Third, the Lord assured Moses that *He felt the burdens of His people and was working on their behalf (6:5; see 2:24)*. God wasn't ignorant of their need or unconcerned about their suffering, nor was He adding to their problems by delaying their deliverance. Everything was working according to His plan and nothing God had planned would fail. Whenever we feel the Lord has abandoned us and doesn't really care, we need to remember His assuring words, "Casting all your care upon Him, for He cares for you" (1 Peter 5:7).

Fourth, *the Lord commanded Moses to speak to Pharaoh again (Ex. 6:9-13)*. Moses reached the depths of discouragement when the Jewish elders wouldn't even listen to him. They had forgotten the signs and promises that Moses and Aaron had given them (4:29-31) and in their anguish were convinced that the situation was hopeless. Moses and the elders had given up, but God hadn't given up on Moses. Moses was still God's servant, and He commissioned him to return to the palace and confront Pharaoh again. In times of despair, it's best to ignore our feelings and simply do what God tells us to do, leaving the consequences with Him.

The genealogy (6:14-27) isn't there by accident, for it's the Lord's way of reminding us, the readers, that *God had prepared Moses and Aaron for their ministry in Egypt*. Their arrival in Jacob's family was part of His providential working. Reuben was Jacob's firstborn, then Simeon, and then Levi, the ancestor of Moses and Aaron. "Before I formed you in the womb I knew you; before you were born I sanctified you; and I ordained you a prophet to the nations" (Jer. 1:5, NKJV). God's calling means God's enabling, and what He begins He always completes (Eph. 2:10; Phil. 1:6).

## 2. Pharaoh belittles God's miracles (Ex. 6:28–8:7)

Up to this point in their confrontation with Pharaoh, Moses and Aaron had simply delivered God's ultimatum. Now the time had come for them to reveal God's power and perform the miraculous signs that proved they were truly sent by God. Still somewhat discouraged, Moses maintained that he wasn't a competent speaker; so God reminded him that Aaron could be his spokesman (6:26–7:2; 4:15-16). However, the Lord advised Moses and Aaron that it would take more than one or two miracles to accomplish His purposes, for He would multiply His signs and wonders in the land of Egypt.

Before we study this remarkable series of miracles, we must focus on the reasons why the Lord took this approach in dealing with Pharaoh and sent these sign judgments to the land of Egypt. The ultimate purpose, of course, was to bring Pharaoh and the Egyptians to their knees so they'd be willing for the Jews to leave the land. But at the same time, the Lord was revealing Himself to both the Israelites and the Egyptians and proving that He alone is God (7:5).

The miracles and plagues were also God's way of judging the gods of Egypt and proving them false and futile. "Against all the gods of Egypt I will execute judgment: I am the Lord" (12:12; and see 18:11 and Num. 33:4). More than eighty different deities were worshiped in Egypt, but they could do nothing to deliver the land and the people from the terrible judgments Jehovah sent. If nothing else, the Egyptians learned that Jehovah was the true and living God.

But the people of Israel also needed to learn this lesson. According to Ezekiel 20:1-9, some of the Jews had begun to worship the Egyptian gods; and when they were delivered from Egypt, they took their gods with them! Did they compro-mise their faith in an attempt to please their captors and receive better treatment? But how could they forsake Jehovah after seeing all the demonstrations of His power? "Our fathers in Egypt did not understand Your wonders; they did not remember the multitude of Your mercies" (Ps. 106:7, NKJV).

*(1) The sign of the serpent (Ex. 7:8-13).* God gave this sign to Moses when He called him in Midian (4:1-5), but now it was Aaron who performed it in Pharaoh's palace. The serpent was one of the special creatures in Egyptian religion, particularly the cobra, which was a symbol of immortality. Aaron's rod became a serpent by the power of the Lord, and his serpent ate up the serpents that the magicians produced.

The three sign miracles that we're considering—the staff turned into a serpent, the water turned to blood, and the inva-sion of the frogs—have in common the fact that all of them were duplicated by Pharaoh's court magicians. Perhaps "coun-terfeited" is a more accurate word, because what they did was more likely deceptive sleight of hand. However, Satan can empower his people to perform "lying wonders" (2 Thes. 2:9-10; Matt. 24:24; Rev. 13:11-15), and that may have been the source of their power.

The Apostle Paul used these Egyptian magicians to teach an important truth: in the last days, Satan will attack God's truth and God's people *by imitating the works of God.* Paul even named two of the court magicians: "Just as Jannes and Jambres opposed Moses, so also these men oppose the truth" (2 Tim. 3:8, NIV). As Jesus taught in the Parable of the Tares (Matt. 13:24-30, 36-43), Satan is a counterfeiter who "plants" imitation Christians in this world. Paul called them "false brethren" (2 Cor. 11:26). Satan has an imitation gospel (Gal. 1:6-9), a counterfeit righteousness (Rom. 10:1-3), and even counterfeit ministers who spread his lies (2 Cor. 11:13-15). Satan will one day produce a false Christ who will deceive the whole world (2 Thes. 2:1-12).

Pharaoh's magicians turned rods into snakes and water into blood, and were also able to produce frogs in the land. Satan opposes God's work by imitating it, and in this way he minimizes the power and glory of God. Pharaoh's attitude was, "Anything Jehovah can do, we can do better!" Of course, he couldn't, but that was enough to bolster his pride and keep him from submitting to the Lord.

*(2) The sign of water turned to blood (Ex. 7:14-25).* This miracle was the first of the ten "plagues" God sent to Egypt, the last of which (the death of the firstborn at Passover) led to the departure of the Jews from Egypt.[7] The word "plague" (9:14; 11:1; 12:13) means "a blow, a stroke," and indicates that the hand of the Lord was punishing the Egyptians.

The longer Pharaoh resisted God, the more serious the judgments became. The first three plagues were distressful (water to blood, frogs, gnats); the second three were painful and costly (flies, death of the livestock, boils); and the last four were dangerous and destructive (hail, locusts, darkness, and the death of the firstborn). The longer sinners resist God's will and refuse to hear His Word, the "louder" He has to speak to them through His judgments.

Not only did the water of the Nile River turn into blood, but so did the other waters in the land and even the water stored in vessels of wood and stone. This was a judgment on the Nile River itself, which was treated like a god, and on Hapi, the god of the Nile, and Isis, the goddess of the Nile. The Nile River was the nation's major source of life-giving water for the people and their crops, so taking away their water supply was a devastating judgment. The people dug wells near the river in order to get pure water, but the fish in the river died and their decay produced a terrible stench. The plague and its consequences lasted a week (7:25).[8]

The magicians used some of the pure well water and duplicated the miracle. But if they had true magical powers, why didn't they reverse the miracle? That would have shown them to be more powerful than Jehovah and would have endeared them to Pharaoh and the people. The answer, of course, is that they didn't have the power to reverse what Moses and Aaron did; the magicians achieved their results by legerdemain and not by any supernatural power.

*(3) The sign of the invasion of frogs (Ex. 8:1-7).* Once more Moses and Aaron commanded Pharaoh "Let my people go!" and warned him that another plague was coming. "Their land brought forth frogs in abundance, in the chambers of their kings" (Ps. 105:30). In Egypt, the frog was a fertility symbol; and Heqet, the goddess of resurrection, fertility, and childbirth, had the head of a frog.

The Lord's warning was very specific. He told Pharaoh that the frogs would go into their houses, beds, ovens and cooking utensils, and would even cling to the bodies of the people. Of course, the magicians again counterfeited the miracle, when the smartest thing they could have done was to nullify it.

## 3. Pharaoh hardens his heart against God (Ex. 8:8-19)

Pharaoh began to harden his heart when Moses and Aaron performed the first miraculous sign before him, just as God said he would do (7:3, 13-14). He hardened his heart further when his magicians counterfeited the signs (v. 22) and even when they couldn't duplicate what Moses and Aaron had done (8:19). When Moses succeeded in stopping the plague of frogs, Pharaoh's heart again hardened (v. 15). This hardening continued throughout the entire series of plagues (v. 32; 9:7, 34-35; 13:15).

What does it mean to harden your heart? It means to see clear evidence of the hand of God at work and still refuse to accept His Word and submit to His will. It means to resist Him by showing ingratitude and disobedience and not having any fear of the Lord or of His judgments. Hardhearted people say with Pharaoh, "Who is the Lord that I should obey His voice?" (5:2)

But the narrative also makes it clear that by sending these various judgments, God was hardening Pharaoh's heart (4:21; 7:3; 9:12; 10:1, 20, 27; 11:10; 14:4, 8, 17). Does this mean that God was unfair and that Pharaoh shouldn't be held responsible for what he did? No, for the same sun that melts the ice also hardens the clay. It all depends on the nature of the material.

To the very end of the contest (14:5ff), Pharaoh was a proud, unrepentant sinner who refused to hear God's Word, do God's will, or even keep his own promises to the Jewish people. The Lord gave him more than enough evidence to convince him that the gods of Egypt were false and the God of the Hebrews was the true and living God. Pharaoh sinned against a flood of light; and though God used him to accomplish His own purposes, Pharaoh made his own decisions and hardened his own heart against God.[9]

*He hardened his heart to God's mercy (Ex. 8:8-15).* Life was miserable for the Egyptians because of the invasion of the frogs, so much so that Pharaoh asked Moses and Aaron to remove the pests. He even admitted that the frogs had been sent by the Lord. So anxious was he to be rid of the frogs that he offered to let the Jewish people go on their worship trip if Moses and Aaron complied with his request. This was only a stratagem to remove the plague, but Moses and Aaron cooperated with him.

Why did Moses let Pharaoh select the time for the frogs to leave? To prove to him and the nation that Jehovah was the living God who heard their words and responded to the prayers of His servants. The plague wasn't a freakish accident; God was in control. But why didn't Pharaoh ask for *immediate* deliverance from the frogs? Why postpone recovery until the next day? Perhaps he was gambling on the chance that the frogs would leave of themselves, and then he wouldn't have to keep his bargain and release the people for their journey. Or, he may have wanted the word to spread that deliverance was coming so that the expectation of the people would be high. The next day the crowds would be waiting and watching, and if Moses failed, Pharaoh was the winner and Jehovah and His servants were discredited.

But Moses wasn't about to fail, for he and Aaron prayed to God that the plague would end. God answered, not by causing the frogs to return to the rivers and ponds, but by killing the frogs and thus forcing the people to carry away the dead bodies and dispose of them. But how do you get rid of piles and piles of dead frogs? It wasn't easy, and the stench only reminded the Egyptians of their king's rebellion against God.

Moses and Aaron kept their promise, and so did the Lord; but Pharaoh refused to keep his word and let the Jewish people go. He really wasn't interested in helping the Israelites; he only wanted to get relief from the awful plague of frogs. Many sinners aren't interested in repenting and receiving God's grace; they want only to be delivered from God's judgment. However, this was only a temporary respite; the greatest judgments were yet to come.

In my pastoral ministry, I've met people who were in trouble in one way or another, who begged me to pray that the Lord would deliver them. They made all kinds of promises to me and to the Lord, telling what they'd do if He would help them. But when He did graciously help them, they forgot their promises and even forgot the Lord. I never saw them again. They were quite unlike the psalmist who wrote: "I will come to Your temple with burnt offerings and fulfill my vows to You — vows my lips promised and my mouth spoke when I was in trouble" (Ps. 66:13-14, NIV).

*He hardened his heart to God's power (Ex. 8:16-19).* In stopping the plague of frogs, God was merciful to Pharaoh; but instead of surrendering to God's mercy, the king only further hardened his heart. So, the Lord sent a third plague and caused the dust of the ground to become gnats.[10] Pharaoh's court magicians couldn't duplicate this miracle and had to admit it was "the finger of God." But even in the face of this evidence, Pharaoh refused to submit to the Lord and only hardened his heart even more. Neither God's mercy nor God's power caused him to repent and obey the Word of the Lord.

The fact that the desert dust became gnats was a judgment against Set, the Egyptian god of the desert. Jehovah was so great that He could give life to insignificant dust and use that life to punish the people who revered Set. But something else was involved. The Egyptians in general, and the priests in particular, were fanatical about cleanliness; and the priests frequently washed and shaved their bodies in order to be acceptable to their gods. Imagine the chagrin and discomfort of the priests when their bodies were invaded by unclean gnats that made life miserable for them! And their gods could do nothing to deliver them!

The defeated magicians saw "the finger of God" in this miracle when it was actually God's "strong hand" (6:1) and "outstretched arm" (6:6). In Scripture, the "finger of God" is also associated with the giving of the Law (31:18; Deut. 9:10), the creation of the heavens (Ps. 8:3), and the casting out of demons (Luke 11:20). All of these are demonstrations of God's authority and power.

But God wasn't through with speaking to Pharaoh or judging the gods of Egypt. Jehovah had seven more plagues to send, and when they were finished, the nation of Egypt would be bankrupt.

"It is a fearful thing to fall into the hands of the living God" (Heb. 10:31).

#### THREE

EXODUS 8:20 – 10:29

# *"The Lord, Mighty in Battle"*

God is gracious and long-suffering, but there comes a time when He will no longer tolerate the disobedience and arrogance of defiant sinners. "To the faithful You show Yourself faithful, to the blameless You show Yourself blameless, to the pure You show Yourself pure, but to the crooked You show Yourself shrewd" (Ps. 18:25-26, NIV). If we walk contrary to Him, He will walk contrary to us (Lev. 26:23-24).

"God shows Himself to each individual according to his character," wrote Charles Spurgeon, and no individual in Scripture illustrates this truth better than the king of Egypt. For months, Moses and Aaron had dealt with Pharaoh, but the king was unwilling to obey God's command or even acknowledge God's authority. The water courses in Egypt had been turned into blood, slimy frogs had invaded the land, and swarms of pesky gnats had irritated the people, but Pharaoh had refused to bend.

What did God do? He declared all-out war on both the ruler of Egypt and the gods of Egypt. The Lord sent six painful and destructive plagues to the land, and then a seventh plague which brought the death of every firstborn son. As you study Pharaoh's responses to these plagues, you see the moral and spiritual deterioration of a man who wouldn't submit to God and paid a terrible price for his rebellion.

Let's consider Pharaoh's responses to the judgments of

God but, at the same time, let's examine our own hearts to learn whether or not we are responding positively to the will of God.

## 1. Bargaining (Ex. 8:20-32)

At certain times of the year, Pharaoh would go to the sacred Nile River to participate in special religious rites, and it certainly must have irritated him on that particular holy occasion to see Moses and Aaron waiting for him. In Pharaoh's eyes, these two men were national nuisances. Actually, Pharaoh was the cause of the nation's troubles, but he would not admit it. God was dealing with Pharaoh in mercy, wanting to bring him into submission; for it's only when we obey God that we can truly enjoy His blessings. With one blow, God could have wiped out Pharaoh and the nation (9:15), but He chose to give them opportunity to repent.

*God's warning (Ex. 8:20-21).* We've already noted that before sending seven of the ten plagues, God warned Pharaoh what was coming but, of course, he refused to believe the Word of God and persisted in his disobedience. The fact that each plague occurred just as God described it, at the time announced, should have convinced Pharaoh and his officers that the God of Israel was in control of these spectacular events. They weren't caused by Pharaoh's magicians, who could neither prevent them nor reverse them, nor were they mere coincidences. The hand of the Lord was against the land of Egypt.

*God's grace (Ex. 8:22).* The Lord added a new feature to this plague by announcing that the Jews in the land of Goshen[1] would escape the plague completely. Only the great God of Israel could control the flight pattern of tiny flies and keep them from entering the land of Goshen. But God's providential care of Israel was evident in all these seven last plagues, because the Jews escaped each one of them (vv. 22-

23; 9:4, 11 ["all the Egyptians"], 26; 10:6 ["all the Egyptians"], 23; 11:7).

Often in Scripture, the land of Egypt symbolizes the world system with its pride and bondage, while the Exodus of Israel from Egypt pictures the deliverance of God's people through the blood of the lamb (John 1:29; Gal. 1:4; 1 Peter 1:18-19). During the time when Joseph was in Egypt, Pharaoh had given the land of Goshen to the Jews, and now God set it apart for His people. In this way God made a "division" between His people and the Egyptians. The word translated "division" in Exodus 8:23 means "a redemption, a ransom, a deliverance." Because they belonged to God in a special way, the Jews were "different" from the Egyptians, but Pharaoh wouldn't acknowledge this fact.[2]

*God's wrath (Ex. 8:24).* Just as God promised, the next day great swarms of flies invaded the land, entering the homes of the people and even the palace of the king. But the flies were more than just an immediate nuisance to the people, for their coming caused some long-range problems as well. The swarms of insects no doubt carried disease germs that affected the people, and it's possible the insects deposited their eggs on the vegetation and the larva that came out ate the plants and thus ruined the land. Some students think that the fly was especially sacred to the Egyptian god Uatchit, so the plague was also God's way of dishonoring another one of the false gods of Egypt.

*Pharaoh's offers (Ex. 8:25-32).* During the time of the plagues, Pharaoh offered four compromises to Moses and Aaron. The first two are recorded here, during the plague of the flies (vv. 25, 28); the third came during the locust plague (10:7-11); and the fourth occurred during the three days of darkness (vv. 24-26). The fact that Pharaoh even thought he could bargain with God is another evidence of his pride. What is mortal man, even the king of a great nation, that he should dare to negotiate the will of God? These offers were all part of Pharaoh's hypocritical scheme to outwit Moses and Aaron, for his heart was still stubborn and unyielding. He wasn't interested in either the will of God or the welfare of the Jews; all he wanted was to stop the plagues.

God's people face similar "Egyptian compromises" today as we seek to serve the Lord. The enemy tells us we don't have to be separated from sin because we can serve God "in the land." God's reply is found in 2 Corinthians 6:14-18. "Don't go too far away," the enemy whispers, "or people will call you a fanatic." James 1:27 and 4:4 demolish that proposal. True service to God means giving Him authority over all our possessions and all the people in our family for whom we're responsible. Not to do so is to disobey Mark 10:13-16; Ephesians 6:4; and Deuteronomy 6:6-13. Once we start to negotiate the will of God and see how close we can get to the world, we have already disobeyed Him in our hearts.

In his first proposal, Pharaoh offered to let the Jews hold their worship feast in the land of Egypt (Ex. 8:25), an offer Moses and Aaron rejected. They knew that some of the animals the Jews would sacrifice were sacred to the Egyptians,[3] and what began as a meeting for solemn worship would quickly turn into a riot. The Jews were a separate people, living in Goshen, a land that had been set apart by God, and they had to separate themselves a three days' journey from Egypt in order to please the Lord.

Pharaoh's second offer was that Israel leave the land but not go too far away (v. 28). The appendix to his offer ("Now pray for me!" NIV) shows that his real concern was to get rid of the swarms of flies. On the surface, it looks like Moses and Aaron accepted this second offer, because Moses promised to get rid of the flies. Perhaps they thought they could travel farther once they got out of the land, but surely they both knew that Pharaoh wouldn't keep his word.

Pharaoh had a habit of begging for help when he needed it (v. 8; 9:28; 10:16-17) and then changing his mind once the plague was removed (8:15, 32; 9:34-35; 10:20). God answered Moses' prayer and removed the flies, but Pharaoh only hardened his heart even more.

## 2. Resisting (Ex. 9:1-12)

As you study the account of the plagues of Egypt, keep in mind the purposes God was fulfilling through these momentous events. First of all, He was manifesting His power to Pharaoh and his officials and proving to them that He alone is the true and living God. At the same time, the Lord was exposing the futility of the Egyptian religion and the vanity of the many gods they worshiped, including Pharaoh himself. All that God did to Egypt was a reminder to His people that their God was fighting for them and they didn't have to worry or be afraid.

*The fifth plague (Ex. 9:1-7).* Moses announced to Pharaoh that unless he released the Israelites within twenty-four hours, all the livestock in the Egyptian fields would be the next target for the demonstration of Jehovah's power. God would send a terrible pestilence upon the horses, donkeys, camels, cattle, sheep, and goats in the fields, and they would die. We don't know what this pestilence was and it's useless to speculate. One thing is sure: God sent the plague and the livestock in the fields perished.[4] Since some of the gods of Egypt were identified with bulls, cows, rams, and other livestock, this judgment was another successful attack on the Egyptian religion.

But God also kept His promise and protected the livestock that belonged to the Jews living in the land of Goshen. When Jacob and his family came to Egypt during the time of Joseph, they brought their flocks and herds with them (Gen. 45:10; 47:1; 50:8). During their time of bondage, the Jews were allowed to keep livestock, for at the Exodus, they took their flocks and herds with them (Ex. 12:37-38).

How did Pharaoh respond to this terrible plague? He hardened his heart and resisted the authority of the Lord. "How blessed is the man who fears always, but he who hardens his heart will fall into calamity" (Prov. 28:14, NASB). The opposite of a hard heart is a heart that fears God, and that reverential fear motivates us to obey the Lord's commands. "The fear of the Lord is the beginning of wisdom" (Prov. 9:10), but the hardhearted person is ignorant of God and His truth (Eph. 4:18).

*The sixth plague (Ex. 9:8-12).* There was no warning given this time. Moses and Aaron simply went to one of the lime-kilns, filled their hands with soot, threw the soot into the air, and trusted God to do the rest. God kept His promise, for wherever the soot landed on the Egyptians and their cattle, it produced painful festering ulcers and boils. Once again, the Jews in Goshen were protected (v. 11).[5]

Pharaoh summoned his court magicians, but they weren't able to go to the palace. The boils had caught up with them and they could do nothing about it! The experience was not only painful but also embarrassing, because the Egyptians were obsessed with physical cleanliness. They took frequent baths, but the festering sores would make that difficult.

The nation of Egypt was being devastated and the people were in great pain, but Pharaoh would not yield. He continued resisting the Lord and His servants, and each act of disobedience only hardened his heart more. "He who is often reproved and hardens his neck, will suddenly be destroyed, and that without remedy" (Prov. 29:1, NKJV). For Pharaoh, the worst was yet to come.

## 3. Deceiving (Ex. 9:13-35)
It didn't look like Moses was achieving his purpose, for each

new plague only made the situation worse. But God was in control and He knew what He was doing. The Lord always has a new word for His servants; all they have to do is listen, believe, and obey.

*A fifth warning (Ex. 9:13-21)*. This is the longest warning so far, perhaps because it introduced the most destructive plague God had sent thus far. Moses again gave God's command that Pharaoh allow the Jewish people to leave the country for a special meeting with the Lord, but this time the Lord added a special warning: the God of the Hebrews was about to release "the full force" of His plagues on Pharaoh, the people, and the land (v. 14, NIV). Pharaoh's heart had become harder, so God's disciplines had to become more severe.

Moses reminded the king of *the Lord's mercy:* "For if by now I had put forth My hand and struck you and your people with pestilence, you would then have been cut off from the earth" (v. 15, NASB). Simply by speaking the word, God could have wiped out the entire Egyptian nation, but God in His mercy doesn't give sinners all that they deserve. How grateful Pharaoh should have been, and yet he continued to resist the Lord.

Moses also reminded Pharaoh of *God's sovereign grace (v. 16)*, a lesson more than one dictator has had to learn the hard way (Dan. 4:28-33; Acts 12:20-24). Apart from the sovereign will of God, Pharaoh would not have been the ruler of Egypt. Each time Pharaoh resisted God, the Lord used the situation to reveal His power and glorify His name. If Pharaoh exalted himself against God, then God exalted Himself through Pharaoh (Ex. 9:17). Paul quoted verse 16 in Romans 9:17 as part of his explanation of the justice and mercy of God with reference to Israel. [6]

The next day, God would send "the worst hailstorm that has ever fallen on Egypt" (Ex. 9:18, NIV), so Moses advised the people to gather into a safe place all the cattle that had not been in the fields and had survived the fifth plague. Even some of Pharaoh's servants now believed God's Word and obeyed it, but the king continued to harden his heart.

*The seventh plague (Ex. 9:22-26).* The next day, Moses stretched his rod toward heaven, and God sent thunder,[7] rain (v. 33), hail, and lightning that ran along the ground. Any person or animal that wasn't under cover was killed, and the plants and trees in the fields were destroyed. Since the flax and barley were ready for harvest (v. 31), the plague must have come in January or February. Once again, the Lord protected His people in the land of Goshen and the plague didn't touch them.

*Another royal lie (Ex. 9:27-35).* Seeing the devastation of his land, Pharaoh quickly summoned Moses and Aaron, something he had done before (8:8) and would do again (10:16). However, this time the proud king acknowledged the justice of God and admitted that he had sinned! (He would do that again. See 10:17.) However, his confession was insincere because it didn't lead to obedience.[8] Moses knew that the king didn't really fear the Lord. All he and his officials wanted to do was stop the terrible hailstorm.

God in His grace answered Moses' prayer and stopped the plague. Pharaoh in his duplicity reneged on his promise and wouldn't let Israel go. When would he ever learn that you can't fight against God and win?

## 4. Appealing (Ex. 10:1-20)

When God gave Moses the instructions for his next meeting with Pharaoh, He added another reason for the great display of His wonders in the plagues: that the Jews might be able to tell the generations to come about the awesome power of their great God.

This purpose was also written into the Passover Feast

(12:26-27; 13:8, 14-15). Whether in the family or the local church, it's good for each new generation to learn and appreciate the way God has worked on behalf of previous generations. Recalling and giving thanks for God's wonderful deeds is one of the basic themes of the Book of Deuteronomy, including what the Lord did to Pharaoh (Deut. 4:34; 7:18-19; 26:5-8; 29:1-3).

*Interrogation (Ex. 10:3-11).* Three questions summarize this confrontation with Pharaoh. First, Moses and Aaron asked Pharaoh how long he was going to persist in his pride and refuse to humble himself before God. It took a great deal of courage to tell any ancient ruler that he was proud, but especially the king of Egypt who was honored as a god. However, Moses and Aaron knew that the Lord would protect them and fulfill His word. They warned Pharaoh that if he failed to obey, vast swarms of locusts would come into the land and destroy everything that hadn't already been destroyed by the hailstorm. Moses and Aaron didn't wait for an answer or another false promise; they delivered their message and walked out of the palace.

The second question came from Pharaoh's officers, "How long shall this man be a snare to us?" (v. 7) They suggested that Pharaoh had been wrong in not letting the Jews go, and they even dared to remind him that his anti-Jewish policy had ruined the land of Egypt. The officers certainly were brave to talk this boldly to Pharaoh, but the nation was in desperate straits and somebody had to do something. What harm could come from the Jewish people temporarily leaving their work and going on their journey?

Pharaoh summoned Moses and Aaron back to the palace and asked the third question: "Who are the ones that are going?" (v. 8, NASB) Moses made it clear that God wanted everybody to take this three-day journey. This included all the men, women, and children, the young and the old, and also the flocks and herds that would be needed to provide sacrifices for the Lord. Pharaoh offered to let only the men go on the journey, knowing that he could hold their families hostage and guarantee their return to Egypt, but it was a compromise that Moses and Aaron rejected.

In his angry response (vv. 10-11), Pharaoh blasphemed the name of God. Literally, he said, "May the Lord be with you if I ever let you and your children go!" *The Living Bible* paraphrases it, "In the name of God I will not let you take your little ones!" Pharaoh interpreted their request as an evil plot to secure their freedom from Egyptian bondage. If all the Jewish men left with their families and livestock, they'd never have to return!

That was the end of the interview, and Pharaoh commanded his officers to drive Moses and Aaron out of the palace. As far as he was concerned, he was finished with Moses and Aaron and would never again listen to their messages from the Lord. However, God had other plans, and before long, Pharaoh would again be appealing for deliverance and relief.

*Invasion (Ex. 10:12-15).* God had seen and heard the entire interview and was prepared to respond to Pharaoh's blasphemy and disobedience. When Moses lifted his rod toward heaven, God sent an east wind that blew for the rest of that day and all through the night. It brought vast swarms of locusts into the land, and they began to devour all the vegetation that had survived the previous plague (9:32). Since the creatures attacked "all the Egyptians" (10:6), the inference is that Israel escaped this devastating plague.

If vocabulary is any indication of significance, then the locust was a significant creature in the Old Testament world, for there are at least eleven different Hebrew words in Scripture referring to it. The Jews were permitted to eat certain species of locusts (Lev. 11:20-23; Deut. 14:19-20; see Matt. 3:1-4), but for the most part, they hated the creatures because of their ability to strip the vegetation from an area with incredible speed. The Israelites used the locust swarm to describe anything that quickly invaded and devastated their land (Jud. 6:5; 7:12; Isa. 33:4; Jer. 46:23; 51:14, 27), and the Prophet Joel compared the locusts to an invading army (Joel 1–2; see Amos 7:1-3).

*Intercession (Ex. 10:16-19).* If Pharaoh's officers thought that Egypt was already ruined (v. 7), then what was their opinion of the situation after the locusts arrived? Within a brief time, no vegetation was left anywhere in the land, and the creatures were invading the houses as well as the fields (v. 6). It was the most devastating natural calamity to hit the land of Egypt in all Egyptian history. In destroying the vegetation, God not only left the land bankrupt, but He triumphed over Osiris, the Egyptian god of fertility and crops. He also proved that He had control over the wind.

Once again Pharaoh sought for relief without repentance, and God mercifully granted his request. God proved His greatness by reversing the winds and carrying all the locusts into the Red Sea. Within a short time, He would put Pharaoh's army into the Red Sea, and then the Israelites would be free to march to their Promised Land.

## 5. Threatening (Ex. 10:21-29)
We don't know how long after the locusts left Egypt that God sent the ninth plague, but the darkness over the land for three days proved that Jehovah was greater than Ra (or Re) and Horus, both of whom the Egyptians revered as sun gods. The darkness wasn't the natural result of a sandstorm but was a miracle from the hand of the God of the Hebrews. There was light for the Israelites in the land of Goshen, just as there would be light for them as they marched out of Egypt (14:19-20). The people of the world (Egypt) walk in the darkness, but the people of God walk in the light (John

3:19-21; 1 John 1:5-10).

Always ready to call for help when he was in trouble, Pharaoh summoned Moses and Aaron and made one more offer. The Jews could go on their journey to worship the Lord, but they couldn't take their flocks and herds with them. Pharaoh's plan was to confiscate all their livestock to replace what he had lost in the plagues, and then send his army to bring the Jews back to Egyptian slavery. Moses and Aaron rejected the offer, not only because they saw through his crafty plan, but because they knew that Israel had to obey all the will of God.

Pharaoh was a proud man, and proud people don't like to be outwitted by those whom they consider their inferiors. Moses and Aaron had refused his four offers and had insisted that he let the Israelites go. These two humble Jews had proved themselves more powerful than the exalted Pharaoh of Egypt, a son of the gods. By His mighty judgments, the God of the Hebrews had brought the great nation of Egypt to its knees; and both the leaders and the common people in the land held Moses in high regard (Ex. 11:3).

Pharaoh was a beaten man, but he wouldn't admit it. Instead, he used his authority to try to intimidate Moses. He warned Moses that if he came back into the palace to see Pharaoh, he would be killed. There were to be no more official audiences before Pharaoh.

But before Moses left the throne room, he delivered God's final warning about the last plague, the death of the firstborn (v. 4). There's an unfortunate chapter division here, for it's likely that Moses delivered his final speech between 10:28 and 29, and then he left the throne room in great anger.[9] Pharaoh had threatened to kill Moses, but God was going to slay every firstborn son in the land of Egypt and then drown Pharaoh's crack troops. In spite of what Pharaoh said about not seeing Moses, on Passover night, Pharaoh would once again call for Moses and plead for his help (12:31).

The hardening of Pharaoh's heart is a warning to all of us. If the sinful human heart doesn't respond by faith to God's Word, it cannot be transformed by the grace of God (Ezek. 36:26-27; Heb. 8:7-13). Instead, it will become harder and harder the longer it resists God's truth. No matter how often God may send affliction, it will only provoke more disobedience. In the last days, when God sends His terrible judgments on the world (Rev. 6–16),[10] people will curse God and continue in their sins, but they will not repent (6:15-17; 9:20-21; 16:9, 11). There will be a whole world full of men and women like Pharaoh who will behold God's judgments and still not repent.

"Today, if you will hear His voice, do not harden your hearts" (Heb. 3:7, NKJV).

"It is a fearful thing to fall into the hands of the living God" (10:31).

# F O U R

## One More Plague

This section of the Book of Exodus focuses on an unpopu-
lar subject: death. King Jehovah (Ps. 95:3) was about to
confront King Pharaoh with another king—death, the "king
of terrors" (Job 18:14). The last enemy, death (1 Cor. 15:26),
would visit Egypt with one last plague and deliver one last
blow to the proud ruler of the land. In one solemn night, all
the firstborn sons and all the firstborn livestock in Egypt
would die, and there would be a great cry throughout the
land (Ex. 11:6; 12:30). Only then would Pharaoh let God's
people go.

However, death wouldn't visit the Jews and their livestock
in the land of Goshen, because the Israelites belonged to the
Lord and were His special people. In the land of Goshen, all
that would die would be innocent yearling lambs, one for
each Jewish household. This night would mark the inauguration of Passover, Israel's first national feast. In this chapter,
we want to examine five different aspects of the Passover
event.

### 1. Passover and the Egyptians (Ex. 11:1-10)
The people of Egypt had been irritated by the first six
plagues, and their land and possessions had been devastated
by the next two plagues. The ninth plague, the three days of
darkness, had set the stage for the most dreadful plague of

48

all, when the messengers of death would visit the land. "He unleashed against them His hot anger, His wrath, indignation and hostility—a band of destroying angels" (Ps. 78:49, NIV).

*Moses heard God's Word (Ex. 11:1-3).* These verses describe what happened before Moses was summoned to the palace to hear Pharaoh's last offer (10:24-29). Moses' speech (11:4-8) was delivered between verses 26 and 27 of chapter 10, and it ended with Moses leaving the palace in great anger (10:29; 11:8).

God told Moses that He would send one more plague to Egypt, a plague so terrible that Pharaoh would not only let the Israelites go but would *command* them to go. Pharaoh would drive them out of the land and thus fulfill the promise God had made even before the plagues had started (6:1; see 12:31-32, 39).

Moses told the Jewish people that the time had come for them to collect their unpaid wages for all the work they and their ancestors had done as slaves in Egypt. The Hebrew word translated "borrow" in the *Authorized Version* simply means "to ask or request." The Jews didn't intend to return what the Egyptians gave them, for that wealth was payment for an outstanding debt that Egypt owed to Israel. God had promised Abraham that his descendants would leave Egypt "with great substance" (Gen. 15:14), and He repeated that promise to Moses (Ex. 3:21-22). God had given His servant Moses great respect among the Egyptians, and now He would give the Jews great favor with the Egyptians, who would freely give their wealth to the Jews (12:36-37).

*Moses warned Pharaoh (Ex. 11:4-10).* This was Moses' final address to Pharaoh, who rejected it just as he did the other warnings. Pharaoh had no fear of God in his heart, therefore, he didn't take Moses' words seriously. But in rejecting God's word, Pharaoh caused the finest young men in the land to die and therefore brought profound sorrow to himself and to his people.

Two questions must be addressed at this point: (1) Why did God slay only the firstborn? (2) Was He just in doing so when Pharaoh was the true culprit? In answering the first question, we also help to answer the second.

In most cultures, firstborn sons are considered special, and in Egypt, they were considered sacred. We must remember that God calls Israel His firstborn son (Ex. 4:22; Jer. 31:9; Hosea 11:1). At the very beginning of their conflict, Moses warned Pharaoh that the way he treated God's firstborn would determine how God treated Egypt's firstborn (Ex. 4:22-23). Pharaoh had tried to kill the Jewish male babies, and his officers had brutally mistreated the Jewish slaves, so in slaying the firstborn, the Lord was simply paying Pharaoh back with his own currency.

Compensation is a fundamental law of life (Matt. 7:1-2), and God isn't unjust in permitting this law to operate in the world. Pharaoh drowned the Jewish babies, so God drowned Pharaoh's army (Ex. 14:26-31; 15:4-5). Jacob lied to his father Isaac (Gen. 27:15-17), and years later, Jacob's sons lied to him (37:31-35). David committed adultery and had the woman's husband murdered (2 Sam. 11), and David's daughter was raped and two of his sons were murdered (2 Sam. 13; 18). Haman built a gallows on which to hang Mordecai, but it was Haman who was hanged there instead (Es. 7:7-10). "Do not be deceived, God is not mocked; for whatever a man sows, that he will also reap" (Gal. 6:7, NKJV).

As to the justice of this tenth plague, who can pass judgment on the acts of the Lord when "righteousness and justice are the foundation of [His] throne"? (Ps. 89:14, NIV) But why should one man's resistance to God cause the death of many innocent young men? However, similar events happen in our world today. How many men and women who died in

50

uniform had the opportunity to vote for or against a declaration of war? And as to the "innocence" of these firstborn sons, only God knows the human heart and can dispense His justice perfectly. "Shall not the Judge of all the earth do right?" (Gen. 18:25)

When you read the Book of Genesis, you learn that God often rejected the firstborn son and chose the next son to carry on the family line and receive God's special blessing. God chose Abel, and then Seth, but not Cain; He chose Shem, not Japheth; Isaac, not Ishmael; and Jacob, not Esau.

These choices not only magnify God's sovereign grace, but they are a symbolic way of saying that our first birth is not accepted by God. We must experience a second birth, a spiritual birth, before God can accept us (John 1:12-13; 3:1-18). The firstborn son represents humanity's very best, but that isn't good enough for a holy God. Because of our first birth, we inherit Adam's sinful nature and are lost (Ps. 51:5-6); but when we experience a second birth through faith in Christ, we receive God's divine nature and are accepted in Christ (2 Peter 1:1-4; Gal. 4:6; Rom. 8:9).

Pharaoh and the Egyptian people sinned against a flood of light and insulted God's mercy. The Lord had endured with much long-suffering the rebellion and arrogance of the king of Egypt as well as his cruel treatment of the Jewish people. God had warned Pharaoh many times, but the man wouldn't submit. Jehovah had publicly humiliated the Egyptian gods and goddesses and proved Himself to be the only true and living God, yet the nation would not believe.

"Because the sentence against an evil work is not executed speedily, therefore the heart of the sons of men is fully set in them to do evil" (Ecc. 8:11, NKJV). God's mercy should have brought Pharaoh to his knees; instead, he repeatedly hardened his heart. Pharaoh's officials humbled themselves before Moses (Ex. 3; 8); why couldn't Pharaoh follow their

example? "Pride goes before destruction, and a haughty spirit before a fall" (Prov. 16:18, NKJV).

## 2. Passover and the Israelites (Ex. 12:1-28, 43-51)

Passover marked a new beginning for the Jews and bound
them together as a nation.[1] When the Lord liberates you
from bondage, it's the dawning of a new day and the beginning of a new life. Whenever you meet the words "redeem"
or "redemption" in the New Testament, they speak of freedom from slavery. (There were an estimated 60 million
slaves in the Roman Empire.) Jewish believers would immediately think of Passover and Israel's deliverance from Egypt
through the blood of the lamb.

The Jewish nation in the Old Testament had two calen-
dars, a civil calendar that began in our September–October,
and a religious calendar that began in our March–April. New
Year's Day in the civil year ("Rosh Hashana"—"beginning of
the year") fell in the seventh month of the religious calendar
and ushered in the special events in the month of Tishri: the
Feast of Trumpets, the Day of Atonement, and the Feast of
Tabernacles. But Passover marked the beginning of the religious year, and at Passover, the focus is on the lamb.

Isaac's question "Where is the lamb?" (Gen. 22:7) introduced one of the major themes of the Old Testament as
God's people waited for the Messiah. The question was ulti-
mately answered by John the Baptist when he pointed to
Jesus and said, "Behold! The Lamb of God who takes away
the sin of the world!" (John 1:29, NKJV) That the Passover
lamb is a picture of Jesus Christ is affirmed in the New
Testament by the Evangelist Philip (Acts 8:32-35; Isa. 53:7-8)
as well as by the Apostles Paul (1 Cor. 5:7), Peter (1 Peter
1:18-20), and John (Rev. 5:5-6; 13:8).[2]

*The lamb was chosen and examined (Ex. 12:1-6a)* on the
tenth day of the month and carefully watched for four days to

make sure it met the divine specifications. There is no question that Jesus met all the requirements to be our Lamb, for the Father said, "This is My beloved Son, in whom I am well pleased" (Matt. 3:17). During the days preceding Passover, our Lord's enemies questioned Him repeatedly, waiting for Him to say something they could attack. During His various trials and interrogations, Jesus was repeatedly questioned, and He passed every test. Jesus knew no sin (2 Cor. 5:21), did no sin (1 Peter 2:22), and in Him there was no sin (1 John 3:5). He's the perfect Lamb of God.

On the fourteenth day of the month, at evening,[3] *the lamb was slain (Ex. 12:6b-7, 12-13, 21-24*) and its blood was applied to the lintel and side posts of the doors of the houses in which the Jewish families lived. It wasn't the *life* of the lamb that saved the people from judgment but the *death* of the lamb. "Without shedding of blood there is no remission" (Heb. 9:22; Lev. 17:11). Some people claim to admire the life and teachings of Jesus who don't want the cross of Jesus; yet it's His death on the cross that paid the price of our redemption (Matt. 20:28; 26:28; John 3:14-17; 10:11; Eph. 1:7; 1 Tim. 2:5-6; Heb. 9:28; Rev. 5:9). Jesus was our substitute; He died our death for us and suffered the judgment of our sin (Isa. 53:4-6; 1 Peter 2:24).

However, to be effective, the blood had to be applied to the doorposts; for God promised, "[W]hen I see the blood, I will pass over you" (Ex. 12:13). It isn't sufficient simply to know that Christ was sacrificed for the sins of the world (John 3:16; 1 John 2:2). We must appropriate that sacrifice for ourselves and be able to say with Paul, "The Son of God loved me, and gave Himself for me" (Gal. 2:20), and with Mary, "My spirit has rejoiced in God my Savior" (Luke 1:46, NKJV). Our appropriation of the Atonement must be personal: "My Lord and my God" (John 20:28).

The Jews dipped flimsy hyssop plants into the basins of

blood and applied the blood to the doorposts (Ex. 12:22). Hyssop was later used to sprinkle the blood that ratified the covenant (24:1-8) and that cleansed healed lepers (Lev. 14:4, 6, 49, 51-52). Our faith may be as weak as the hyssop, but it's not faith in our faith that saves us, but faith in the blood of the Savior.

*The lamb was roasted and eaten (Ex. 12:8-11, 46)*, and the eating was done in haste, each family member ready to move out when the signal was given. The meal consisted of the roasted lamb, unleavened bread, and bitter herbs, each of which symbolized an important spiritual truth.

In order that the lamb might be kept whole, it was roasted in the fire and not boiled in water. It's not likely that the Jews had vessels large enough for boiling a whole lamb, but even if they did, it was forbidden. The bones would have to be broken and the meat in cooking would separate from the bones. The bones were not to be broken nor were pieces of meat to be carried outside the house (v. 46; John 19:31-37; Ps. 34:20). It was important to see the wholeness of the lamb.

We trust Christ that we might be saved from our sins by His sacrifice, but we must also feed on Christ in order to have strength for our daily pilgrim journey. As we worship, meditate on the Word, pray, and believe, we appropriate the spiritual nourishment of Jesus Christ and grow in grace and knowledge.[4]

Along with the lamb, *the Israelites ate bitter herbs and unleavened bread (Ex. 12:14-20, 39; 13:3-7)*. Tasting the bitter herbs would remind the Jews of their years of bitter bondage in the land of Egypt. However, when circumstances became difficult during their wilderness journey, the people usually recalled "the good old days" and wanted to go back to Egypt (16:3; 17:1-3; Num. 11:1-9; 14:1-5). They forgot the bitterness of their servitude in that horrible iron furnace.

Their bread was unleavened (without yeast) for two reasons: there wasn't time for the bread to rise (Ex. 12:39), and leaven was a symbol of impurity to the Jews. For a week after Passover, they were required to eat unleavened bread and to remove every trace of leaven from their dwellings.

Yeast is an image of sin: it's hidden; it works silently and secretly; it spreads and pollutes; and it causes dough to rise ("puffed up"—1 Cor. 4:18–5:2). Both Jesus and Paul compared false teaching to yeast (Matt. 16:6-12; Mark 8:15; Gal. 5:1-9), but it's also compared to hypocrisy (Luke 12:1) and sinful living (1 Cor. 5:6-8). Paul admonishes local churches to purge out the sin from their midst and present themselves as an unleavened loaf to the Lord.

If any meat was left over from the feast, it had to be burned. The lamb was so special that it couldn't be treated like ordinary food. In a similar way, the manna was special and couldn't be hoarded from day to day, except for the day before the Sabbath (Ex. 16:14-22).

*They ate as families and as a congregation (Ex. 12:25-28; 13:8-10)*. The meal was prepared for the family (see Ex. 12:3-4) and was to be eaten by the family members. God's concern is for the entire family and not just for the parents. If the precious Jewish children were not protected by the blood and strengthened by the food, they couldn't be delivered from Egypt, and that would be the end of the nation.[5]

Though there were many Jewish households in the land of Goshen, God saw all of them as one congregation (vv. 3, 6). When local Christian congregations today meet to celebrate the Lord's Supper, God sees each individual assembly as part of one body, the church. That's why Paul could write about "the whole building . . . the whole family . . . the whole body" (Eph. 2:21; 3:15; 4:16, NKJV). Israel was one nation because of the blood of the lamb, and the church is one fellowship because of Jesus Christ.

Not only was the Passover supper an ordinance to be

obeyed (Ex. 12:14, 17, 24, 43), but it was also a "memorial" to be celebrated to keep alive in Israel the story of the Exodus (v. 14; 13:8-10). After Israel had entered and conquered the Promised Land, it would be easy for the people to settle down and forget the great acts of God on their behalf. The annual observance of Passover would give Jewish parents another opportunity to teach their children the meaning of their freedom and what God did for them. The adults were to be "living links" with Israel's past so that each new generation would understand what it meant to be a member of God's chosen nation. (See Deut. 6:1-15; 11:18-21; Pss. 34:11; 78:1-7; 145:4.)

In later years, orthodox Jews took Exodus 13:8-9 and 16 literally, along with Deuteronomy 6:8-9 and 11:18. Moses said that Passover was to be "like a sign" (see Ex. 13:9, NIV), that is, a reminder to them of what the Lord had done. Instead, the orthodox interpreted this to mean that the Jewish men were to wear the Scriptures on their person. So, they wrote Scripture passages on parchment and put them into little boxes which they wore on the left arm and the forehead. In the New Testament, they are called "phylacteries" (see Matt. 23:5).[6]

Eating the feast was *forbidden to those outside the covenant (Ex. 12:43-51)*. Not only did a "mixed multitude" join with Israel when they left Egypt (v. 38), but the Jews would encounter many different nations on their march and when they reached Canaan.

Israel might be tempted to let their Gentile neighbors join with them in celebrating Passover, their "national independence day," but the Lord prohibited this practice. Later, He would forbid the Jews from joining with their neighbors in their pagan religious ceremonies, for Israel was to be a separated people (Deut. 7:1-11).[7]

Who were these "foreigners" whom God said the

Israelites couldn't invite to the Passover celebration? They were non-Israelites who had never been circumcised and therefore were not children of the covenant. They might be slaves in the camp of Israel or simply strangers (resident aliens) living among the Jews. Any stranger or servant could submit to circumcision and become a part of the nation and share the covenant privileges, but they also had to accept the responsibilities.

### 3. Passover and the Lord (Ex. 12:29-42, 51)

We usually call this event "the Jewish Passover," but the Bible calls it "the Lord's Passover" (vv. 11, 27; Lev. 23:5; Num. 28:16). The observance was more than an "Independence Day" celebration, because the feast was kept "unto the Lord" (Ex. 12:48; Num. 9:10, 14). "It is the sacrifice of the Lord's passover" (Ex. 12:27). The focus of attention is on the Lord because what occurred that special night was because of Him. At least seventeen times in Exodus 12 "the Lord" is mentioned because He was the one in charge.

*God revealed His power (Ex. 12:29-30)*. After the Jews held their Passover feast "between the evenings," they waited for God's signal to depart. At midnight, the Lord struck the first-born, death visited every Egyptian household, and a great cry arose throughout Egypt (11:6; 12:30). Death is no respecter of persons, and that night it touched the family of the lowest Egyptian prisoner as well as Pharaoh himself. However, not a single death occurred among the Jewish people in the land of Goshen. The lesson here is obvious: Unless you're protected by the blood of Christ, when death comes, you'll be completely unprepared, and *you don't know when death is coming.*

*God kept His promises (Ex. 12:31-36)*. God told Moses what was going to happen and Moses announced it to Pharaoh (11:1-8), but Pharaoh didn 't believe it. However,

God's word didn't fail. Just as He said to Moses, the firstborn in Egypt died, there was a great cry in Egypt, Pharaoh told the Israelites to leave, and the Egyptian people freely gave them of their wealth. Promises were fulfilled that night that were made to Abraham centuries before (Gen. 15:13-14). "There has not failed one word of all His good promise, which He promised through His servant Moses" (1 Kings 8:56, NKJV).

*God delivered His people (Ex. 12:37-42, 51).* The Israelites marched boldly out of Egypt in full view of the Egyptians who were busy burying their dead (Num. 33:3-4). If there were about 600,000 Jewish men taking part in the Exodus, then the total number of Jews must have been about 2 million. Like an army with its divisions (Ex. 12:17, 51), they marched quickly in orderly fashion, with their flocks and their herds. Not one Jew was too feeble to march, and the Egyptians were glad to see the Jews get out of their land (Ps. 105:37-38).

Two different words are used to describe what the *King James Version* calls "the mixed multitude" that left Egypt with the Jews. In Exodus 12:38, the word is simply a "swarm" or "multitude," while in Numbers 11:4, it's "rabble" (see NIV). This suggests that the "mixed multitude" originated most of the complaining in the camp that created so many problems for Moses. Some of this crowd may have been Egyptians who had married Jews, contrary to God's law; others were probably Egyptians who were frightened, impressed with Jehovah's power (Ex. 9:20), and wanted to benefit from being with God's chosen people. Perhaps they thought more judgments might fall on the land and they wanted to escape them.

Whoever they were, this "mixed multitude" represents those in this world who outwardly identify with God's people but inwardly are not truly the children of God. They might be church members and even religious leaders, but their attitudes and appetites are radically different from those who truly belong to the Lord. Jesus warned, "Not everyone who says to Me 'Lord, Lord,' shall enter the kingdom of heaven, but he who does the will of My Father in heaven" (Matt. 7:21, NKJV). Great multitudes followed Jesus during His earthly ministry, but He wasn't impressed with these crowds. See Matthew 13:1-9, 18-23; Luke 14:25-35; and John 6:60-71.

God's promises are never in error and His timing is never wrong (Ex. 12:40-41). The Exodus took place 480 years before the fourth year of Solomon's reign (1 Kings 6:1), which was the year 966 B.C. That means that the date of the Exodus was 1446 B.C. and that Jacob's descendants had been in Egypt since 1876 B.C. Both Genesis 15:13 and Acts 7:6 give "four hundred years," which is a round figure, but Galatians 3:17 specifies "430 years." Most conservative biblical scholars accept 1446 as the date of the Exodus.

Israel's exodus from Egypt is mentioned many places in Scripture as the greatest demonstration of Jehovah's power in the history of Israel. The prophets point to the Exodus as proof of God's love for Israel (Jer. 2:1-8; Hosea 11:1). They also refer to the Exodus when they speak about the Jews' deliverance from Babylonian Captivity (Jer. 16:14; 23:7-8). Isaiah promises a future regathering of Israel to their land and compares it to the Exodus (Isa. 11:15; 43:14-21; 51:9-11). Frequently, Isaiah mentions a "highway" that will facilitate this future exodus of the Jews from the Gentile nations (11:16; 19:23; 35:8; 62:10).

**4. Passover and the firstborn (Ex. 13:1-16)**
This section explains the significance of the firstborn in the nation of Israel. Not only once a year at Passover were the Jews reminded of God's grace and power, but each time a

firstborn male, man or beast, came into the world, that first-born issue had to be redeemed. Because of God's mighty acts in protecting and redeeming His people and saving the firstborn of humans and livestock from death (12:12-13), all the firstborn belonged to God. They were sanctified, that is, set apart for God's exclusive possession.

This ordinance of redemption would take effect when the Jews were in the Promised Land, and later Moses explained how to do it (Lev. 12; Num. 18:14-19). The firstborn of an ass, being an unclean animal, could not be sacrificed to God, so it was redeemed by a lamb. Being a valuable work animal, the ass was spared only in this way, but if the animal was not redeemed, then it had to be killed. Parents would bring their firstborn sons to the Lord and offer the appropriate sacrifice (Lev. 12:6-8). When Mary and Joseph came to the temple to redeem the Redeemer, they brought the humble sacrifice of the poor (Luke 2:21-24).

When a firstborn son was redeemed, or a firstborn animal, it gave adults the opportunity to explain how God had rescued the firstborn in the land of Goshen on Passover night, and how He had slain all the Egyptian firstborn, both humans and livestock. Even though he had nothing to do with the birth order in the home, each firstborn son in a Jewish family was very special to the parents and to the Lord.

## 5. Passover and Moses (Heb. 11:27-29)
We must never forget that it was the once timid and excuse-making Moses who, with his brother Aaron, confronted Pharaoh time after time and finally conquered Pharaoh and all the power of Egypt. Hebrews 11 reminds us that Moses accomplished all of this by faith in the living God. Passover and the Exodus are memorials to the power of faith.

Hebrews 11:27 refers to Exodus 10:28-29 when Pharaoh

threatened to kill Moses if he came to see him one more time. Moses believed God's promises and had no fear of what the king might do. Faith simply means that we rely on God and obey His Word, regardless of feelings, circumstances, or consequences. By faith, Moses kept the Passover, even though slaying the lambs and putting the blood on the doors looked ridiculous to the Egyptians and was certainly offensive to them. At any time, Pharaoh could have sent his officers to Moses and killed him, but God kept him safe.

It was faith in God's word that had brought Moses back to Egypt to lead his people; it was faith that took him out of Egypt; and it was faith that separated him and his people from Egypt as they crossed the Red Sea. No matter what our circumstances may be, we can trust God to bring us out and take us through.

Jesus established the Lord's Supper after He had led His disciples in celebrating Passover, for He is the fulfillment of the Passover as the Lamb of God who died for the sins of the world. Each time we share in the Lord's Supper, we look back and remember His death, but we also look ahead and anticipate His coming again. When Jesus returns, a wonderful exodus will take place! The dead in Christ will be raised and the living believers will be caught up with them and taken to heaven to be with the Lord (1 Thes. 4:13-18).

Hallelujah, what a Savior!

# FIVE

# *Redeemed and Rejoicing*

"History does not long entrust the care of freedom to the weak or the timid."

President Dwight D. Eisenhower spoke those words in his first inaugural address, January 20, 1953. As the man who helped lead the Allies to victory in World War II, General Eisenhower knew a great deal about the high cost of victory as well as the heavy burden of freedom that always follows. British novelist Charles Kingsley rightly said, "There are two freedoms — the false, where a man is free to do what he likes; and the true, where a man is free to do what he ought." Throughout their history, the nation of Israel struggled with both of these freedoms, just as God's people struggle with them today.

It's a mark of maturity when we learn that freedom is a tool to build with, not a toy to play with, and that freedom involves accepting responsibility. Israel's exodus experience taught them that their future success lay in fulfilling three important responsibilities: following the Lord (13:17-22), trusting the Lord (14:1-31), and praising the Lord (15:12-21).

## 1. Following the Lord (Ex. 13:17-22)
Israel's exodus from Egypt wasn't the end of their experience with God; it was the new beginning. "It took one night

to take Israel out of Egypt, but forty years to take Egypt out of Israel," said George Morrison.[1] If Israel obeyed His will, God would bring them into the Promised Land and give them their inheritance. Forty years later, Moses would remind the new generation, "He [the Lord] brought you out of Egypt . . . to bring you in, to give you [the] land as an inheritance" (Deut. 4:37-38, NKJV).

The same thing can be said of the redemption we have in Christ: God brought us out of bondage that He might bring us into blessing. A.W. Tozer used to remind us that "we are saved *to* as well as saved *from*."[2] The person who trusts Jesus Christ is born again into the family of God, but that's just the beginning of an exciting new adventure that should lead to growth and conquest. God liberates us and then leads us through the varied experiences of life, a day at a time, so that we might get to know Him better and claim by faith all that He wants us to have. At the same time, we come to know ourselves better; we discover our strengths and weaknesses, and we grow in understanding God's will and trusting His promises.

*God plans the route for His people (Ex. 13:17-18)*. Nothing takes God by surprise, for in His providence He plans the best way for His people to take. We may not always understand the way He chooses, or even agree with it, but His way is always the right way. We may confidently say, "He leads me in the paths of righteousness for His name's sake" (Ps. 23:3, NKJV), and we should humbly pray, "Show me Your ways, O Lord; teach me Your paths. Lead me in Your truth and teach me" (25:4-5, NKJV).

If there had been any military strategists in Israel that night, they probably would have disagreed with the evacuation route God selected because it was too long.[3] Israel's immediate destination was Mt. Sinai, but why take several million people the long way instead of using the shorter and easier route? The answer is: because there were Egyptian military posts along the shorter route, and the soldiers stationed there would have challenged the Jews. Furthermore, crossing the Philistine borders would have invited their army to attack, and the last thing Israel needed was a war with the neighbors. God knew what He was doing when He chose the longer way.

If you permit the Lord to direct your steps (Prov. 3:5-6), expect to be led occasionally on paths that may seem unnecessarily long and circuitous. Remind yourself that God knows what He's doing, He isn't in a hurry, and as long as you follow Him, you're safe and in the place of His blessing. He may close some doors and suddenly open others, and we must be alert (Acts 16:6-10; 2 Cor. 2:12-13).

*God encourages His people's faith (Ex. 13:19).* Before he died, Joseph made his brothers promise that, when God delivered Israel from Egypt, their descendants would take his coffin with them to the Promised Land (Gen. 50:24-25; Heb. 11:22). Joseph knew that God would keep His promise and rescue the Children of Israel (15:13-16). Joseph also knew that he belonged in the land of Canaan with his people (49:29-33).

What did this coffin mean to the generations of Jews who lived during the years of terrible bondage in Egypt? Certainly the Jews could look at Joseph's coffin and be encouraged. After all, the Lord cared for Joseph during his trials, and finally delivered him, and He would care for the nation of Israel and eventually set them free. During their years in the wilderness, Israel saw Joseph's coffin as a reminder that God has His times and keeps His promises. Joseph was dead, but he was bearing witness to the faithfulness of God. When they arrived in their land, the Jews kept their promise and buried Joseph with Abraham, Isaac, and Jacob (Josh. 24:32).

64

Is it idolatrous to have visible reminders of God's faithfulness? Not necessarily, for you find several significant monuments in the Book of Joshua. When Israel crossed the Jordan River, they put up a monument of stones on the farther shore to commemorate what God had done (Josh. 4). They also put stones on Mt. Ebal and Mt. Gerizim to remind them of God's Law (Ex. 8:30-35). A heap of stones bore witness of Achan's treachery (Josh. 7:25-26), and a "witness stone" was a reminder of Israel's rededication after the conquest of the land (24:24-28). Samuel set up a stone to commemorate Israel's victory over the Philistines and called it "Ebenezer, the stone of help" (1 Sam. 7:12).

As long as we keep obeying the Lord, such reminders can encourage our faith. The important thing is that they point to the Lord and not to a dead past, and that we continue to walk by faith and obey the Lord today.

*God goes before His people to lead the way (Ex. 13:20-22).* The nation was guided by a pillar (column) of cloud by day that became a pillar of fire by night. This pillar was identified with the angel of the Lord who led the nation (14:19; 23:20-23; see Neh. 9:12). God occasionally spoke from the pillar of cloud (Num. 12:5-6; Deut. 31:15-16; Ps. 99:7), and the pillar of cloud also shielded the people from the hot sun as they journeyed by day (105:39). When the cloud moved, the camp moved; when the cloud waited, the camp waited (Ex. 40:34-38).

We don't have this same kind of visible guidance today, but we do have the Word of God which is a light (Ps. 119:105) and a fire (Jer. 23:29). It's interesting to note that the pillar of fire gave light to the Jews but was darkness to the Egyptians (Ex. 14:20). God's people are enlightened by the Word (Eph. 1:15-23), but the unsaved can't understand God's truth (Matt. 11:25; 1 Cor. 2:11-16).

The Spirit of God, who is the Spirit of Truth, guides us by

teaching us the Word (John 16:12-13). Just as God spoke to Moses from the pillar, so the Lord communicates with us from the Scriptures by making them clear to us. There are times when we aren't sure which way God wants us to go, but if we wait on Him, He will eventually guide us.

How foolish it would have been for the Jews to pause in their march and take a vote to see which route they should take to Mt. Sinai! Certainly there's a place for community counsel and referendum (Acts 6:1-7), but when God has spoken, there's no need for consultation. On more than one occasion in Scripture, the majority has been wrong.

## 2. Trusting the Lord (Ex. 14:1-31)

"He [God] made known His ways to Moses, His acts to the children of Israel" (Ps. 103:7, NKJV). The Jewish people were told what God wanted them to do, but Moses was told why God was doing it. "The secret of the Lord is with them that fear Him" (25:14). The leadership of Moses was a key ingredient in Israel's success.

*Egypt's pursuit (Ex. 14:1-9).* It dawned on Pharaoh and his officers that, by allowing their Jewish slaves to escape, they had threatened, if not destroyed, Egypt's whole economy, so the logical thing was to go after the Jews and bring them back. Now we're given another reason why the Lord selected this route: the reports would convince Pharaoh that the Jews were wandering like lost sheep in the wilderness and therefore were fair game for his army to pursue and capture. The Lord was drawing the Egyptians into His trap.

What seemed like an easy victory to Egypt would turn out to be an ignominious defeat, and the Lord would get all the glory. Once again He would triumph over Pharaoh and the gods and goddesses of Egypt. Pharaoh commandeered all the chariots of Egypt, mounted his own royal chariot, and pursued the people of Israel.

*Israel's panic (Ex. 14:10-12).* As long as the Israelites kept their eyes on the fiery pillar and followed the Lord, they were walking by faith and no enemy could touch them. But when they took their eyes off the Lord and looked back and saw the Egyptians getting nearer, they became frightened and began to complain.

These verses introduce the disappointing pattern of Israel's behavior during their march from Egypt to Canaan. As long as everything was going well, they usually obeyed the Lord and Moses and made progress. But if there was any trial or discomfort in their circumstances, they immediately began to complain to Moses and to the Lord and asked to go back to Egypt. However, before we criticize the Jews, perhaps we'd better examine our own hearts. How much disappointment or discomfort does it take to make us unhappy with the Lord's will so that we stop believing and start complaining? "For we walk by faith, not by sight" (2 Cor. 5:7).

When you forget God's promises, you start to imagine the worst possible scenario. The Jews were sure that they and their children would die in the wilderness as soon as Pharaoh's army caught up with them. The frightened people reminded Moses that they had told him to leave them alone (Ex. 5:20-23), but he had persisted in challenging Pharaoh. Israel was now in a terrible predicament, and Moses was to blame. Unbelief has a way of erasing from our memory all the demonstrations we've seen of God's great power and all the instances we know of God's faithfulness to His Word.

*God's power (Ex. 14:13-31).* Moses was a man of faith who knew that Pharaoh's army was no threat to Jehovah. He gave several commands to the people, and the first was, "Fear not" (v. 13).[4] Sometimes fear energizes us and we quickly try to avoid danger, but sometimes fear paralyzes us and we don't know what to do. Israel was tempted to flee, so Moses gave his second command: "Stand still, and see the salvation of the Lord" (v. 13). By faith the Jews had marched out of Egypt, and now by faith they would stand still and watch God destroy the Egyptian charioteers.

Moses not only told them to stand still, but also to "be still" (v. 14). How easy it would have been to weep, complain, and keep criticizing Moses, but none of those things would have helped them out of their predicament. Unbelief complains, but faith obeys and brings glory to the Lord. "Be still, and know that I am God" (Ps. 46:10). What is there to complain about when we have the wonderful promise, "The Lord shall fight for you"? (Ex. 14:14) Later in their journey, the Lord would help Joshua and the Jewish army fight their battles (17:8); but this time, God would defeat the Egyptians without Israel's assistance.

The next order came from God to Moses, "Go forward!" (v. 15) The fact that Israel was facing the sea was no problem to God, and He told Moses exactly what to do. When Moses lifted up his rod, the waters would part, and Israel would be able to walk across on dry land and escape the Egyptian army. At Moses' signal, the waters would then flow back, drown the Egyptian soldiers, and prevent Israel from returning to Egypt. In the years that followed, each time the Jews expressed a desire to return to Egypt, they should have remembered that God closed the waters and locked the door.

Why did God perform this series of miracles for the Jewish people? They certainly didn't deserve it as they stood there cringing in fear and complaining that God didn't seem to know what He was doing. To begin with, He was keeping His promise that He would deliver Israel and take them as His people (3:7-8). In years to come, pious Jews would measure everything by the demonstration of God's great power at the Exodus. But God had another purpose in mind: revealing once more His power and glory in the defeat of the

Egyptian army. "And the Egyptians shall know that I am the Lord" (14:18).

The pillar moved between the Israelites and the Egyptians, indicating that God had become a wall of protection between His people and their enemies. The pillar gave light to Israel but darkness to the enemy, for the faithless people of Egypt couldn't understand the ways of God. When Moses stretched out his hand, the Lord sent a powerful wind that drove the sea waters back and opened the way for the Jews to cross. Psalm 77:16-20 indicates that a severe rainstorm accompanied the high winds, and after Israel had crossed, the rain turned Israel's dry pathway into a muddy road. When the Egyptian soldiers tried to follow, the mud disabled their chariots and impeded their progress and when the waters returned, all the Egyptian soldiers were drowned. It was indeed a night to be remembered.

Knowing that the enemy was in pursuit, and hearing the wind blowing all night, the Israelites must have wondered what was going to happen and why God was taking so long. But when we have faith in God's promises, we have peace in our hearts. "Why are you so fearful?" Jesus asked His disciples after He had calmed a storm. "How is it that you have no faith?" (Mark 4:40, NKJV) Faith and fear can't live together in the same heart, for one will destroy the other. True faith depends on what God says, not on what we see or how we feel. It has well been said that faith is not believing in spite of evidence—that's superstition—but obeying in spite of consequence.

This series of divine miracles was certainly a revelation of the greatness and power of God, His faithfulness to His promises, and His concern for His people. Future psalmists would extol the Lord for His mighty works at the Red Sea (Pss. 66; 78; 80–81; 105–106; 136), and the prophets would use the Exodus to encourage the Jewish exiles in their return to their land after the Babylonian Captivity (Isa. 43:1-7; 52:11-12; 55:12-13; Jer. 16:14-15; 23:7-8), as well as to motivate the backslidden nation to return to the Lord (Jer. 2:2-3; Ezek. 20; Hosea 2:14-23; Amos 3; Micah 6:3-4).[5]

*Moses' position (Ex.14:31; 1 Cor. 10:1-2).* Paul saw Israel's march through the sea as a "baptism," for the water was on either side like a wall and the cloud of God's presence was behind them and over them. As it were, Israel was "immersed" as they quickly crossed the dry bed of the sea. Their deliverance was certainly the act of God, but it was accomplished through the obedient leadership of Moses. As a result, "the people . . . believed the Lord and His servant Moses" (Ex. 14:31). They were now constituted as a nation with Moses as their leader. Through this "baptism," the people of Israel were identified with Moses, just as in water baptism God's people today are identified with Jesus Christ. The miracle of the Exodus became a part of Israel's confession of faith when they brought their gifts to the Lord (Deut. 26:1-11).

## 3. Praising the Lord (Ex. 15:1-21)

With their enemies drowned and their freedom secure, the people of Israel burst into song and praised the Lord. We don't read that they praised God while they were enslaved in Egypt, and while they were going out of the land, they were complaining to Moses and asking him to let them go back. But it takes maturity for God's people to have a "song in the night" (Job 35:10; Ps. 42:8; Matt. 26:30; Acts 16:25), and the Jews were very immature in their faith at that time.

This hymn of praise has four stanzas: God's victory is announced (Ex. 15:1-5), God's weapons are described (vv. 6-10), God's character is extolled (vv. 11-16a), and God's promises are fulfilled (vv. 16b-18).

*God's victory is announced (Ex. 15:1-5).* The Lord is mentioned ten times in this hymn as Israel sang to the Lord and about the Lord, for true worship involves faithful witness to who God is and what He has done for His people.

God's victory was a glorious victory, for it was wholly the work of the Lord. The Egyptian army was thrown into the sea (vv. 1 and 4), and the soldiers sank like stones (v. 5) and like lead (v. 10). They were consumed like burning stubble (v. 7). Pharaoh had ordered the Jewish boy babies to be drowned, so God paid him back in kind and drowned his troops.

The statement "The Lord is a man of war" (v. 3) may upset people who feel that anything relating to warfare is alien to the Gospel and the Christian life. Some denominations have taken the "militant" hymns out of their hymnals, including "Onward Christian Soldiers." But Moses promised the people, "The Lord shall fight for you" (14:14; see Deut. 1:30); and one of God's names is "Jehovah-Sabaoth," which means "Lord of hosts, Lord of armies," a title that's used 285 times in the Old Testament. Martin Luther wrote in his Reformation hymn "A Mighty Fortress Is Our God":

> Did we in our own strength confide,
> Our striving would be losing,
> Were not the right Man on our side,
> The Man of God's own choosing.
> Dost ask who that may be?
> Christ Jesus, it is He;
> Lord Sabaoth His name,
> From age to age the same,
> And He must win the battle.

If there is in this world an enemy like Satan, and if sin and evil are hateful to God, then He must wage war against them. "The Lord will march out like a mighty man; like a warrior

He will stir up His zeal; with a shout He will raise the battle
cry and will triumph over His enemies" (Isa. 42:13, NIV).
Jesus Christ is both the Lamb who died for our sins and the
Lion who judges sin (Rev. 5:5-6), and one day He will ride
forth to conquer His enemies (19:11). To emphasize only
"God is love" (1 John 4:8, 16) and eliminate "God is light"
(1 John 1:5) is to rob God of His attributes of righteousness,
holiness, and justice.

On three special occasions recorded in Scripture, the Jews
sing, "The Lord is my strength and song, and He is become
my salvation" (Ex. 15:2): when God delivered Israel from
Egypt, when the Jewish remnant laid the foundation of the
second temple (Ps. 118:14),[6] and when the Jews are regath-
ered and return to their land to enjoy the blessings of the
kingdom (Isa. 12:2).[7] In each instance, the Lord gives
strength, salvation, and a song.[8]

*God's weapons are described (Ex. 15:6-10).* "The Lord is a
man of war" who doesn't fight with conventional weapons.
Using human characteristics to describe divine attributes,[9]
the singers declare that His right hand is glorious in power,
His majesty throws His opponents down, and His anger con-
sumes them like fire eats up stubble. The breath from His
nostrils is the wind that blew back the waters and congealed
them so they stood like a wall. When the overconfident
Egyptian soldiers thought to catch up with the Jews, God
simply breathed and the waters returned and drowned the
army. What a mighty God is He!

*God's character is extolled (Ex. 15:11-16a).* In the ten
plagues that He sent on the land, the Lord had already
proved Himself greater than the gods and goddesses of
Egypt. No wonder His people sang, "Who is like unto Thee,
O Lord, among the gods?" (v. 11; see Micah 7:18) The
answer, of course, is nobody, for no other being in the universe is "majestic in holiness, awesome in glory, working

wonders" (Ex. 15:11, NIV). This stanza goes on to praise God for His power (v. 12), His mercy to deliver, His wisdom to guide (v. 13), and the awesomeness of His person to bring fear to the hearts of His enemies (v. 14).

The nation anticipated their march to the Promised Land, knowing that the news of the Exodus would travel quickly to the other nations and bring fear to the hearts of their enemies (vv. 14-16a). When the spies entered Jericho, they discovered that the people of the land were indeed paralyzed with fear as Israel arrived on the scene (Josh. 2:8-13, 24; see Num. 22:3; Ps. 114). The heathen nations knew that the true and living God was more powerful than their gods and would give Israel the victory.

*God's promise is fulfilled (Ex. 15:16b-18).* This stanza looks forward to Israel's conquest of Canaan and points out that God purchased Israel and they are His people. The nations in Canaan would be as still and dead as stones as the Jewish army conquered the land and the tribes claimed their inheritance. God brought them out of Egypt that He might bring them into Canaan and plant them in their own land (Pss. 44:2; 80:8, 15; Isa. 5). God would put His sanctuary among His people and dwell with them in glory. "The Lord shall reign forever and ever" (Ex. 15:18) is the climax of the song, emphasizing that God is sovereign and eternal.

When you read verse 19 in the *Authorized Version,* you get the impression that Pharaoh himself accompanied his army and led them into the sea where they all drowned, but the NASB clears up this misunderstanding. It reads, "For the horses of Pharaoh with his chariots and his horsemen went into the sea." Pharaoh was apparently on the scene (14:6), but he certainly wasn't leading the army.

Not only did Moses lead the men in the singing of this anthem of praise (15:1), but Miriam[10] formed a special choir of Jewish women who assisted her as she repeated the first words of the song. Their joyful enthusiasm was expressed as they sang, played their tambourines, and danced before the Lord (see 1 Sam. 18:6; 2 Sam. 1:20). Miriam is called "the prophetess," which explains why later she had the courage to criticize Moses (Num. 12:1-2).[11]

"And the waters covered their enemies; there was not one of them left. Then believed they His words; they sang His praise" (Ps. 106:11-12). However, that isn't the end of the story, for the nation's singing soon turned into complaining as they entered the wilderness and headed toward Mt. Sinai. "They soon forgot His works; they waited not for His counsel, but lusted exceedingly in the wilderness, and tempted God in the desert" (Ps. 106:13-14).

It wasn't easy for them to carry the burden of freedom, and God had to teach them how to live a day at a time.

EXODUS 15:22–16:36

# *The School of Life*

Do not pray for easy lives. Pray to be stronger men and women. Do not pray for tasks equal to your powers. Pray for powers equal to your tasks."

That wise counsel comes from American preacher and Episcopal bishop Phillips Brooks (1835–1893). When he spoke those words to his Boston congregation, perhaps he had the people of Israel in mind, for whenever the going got tough, the Israelites began grumbling and talking about returning to Egypt. It was one thing for the Jews to stand by the Red Sea and joyfully sing praises to the Lord, and quite something else to trust God in their daily wilderness walk. They were no different from God's people today. Life is still a school, and the painful experiences of life teach us some of the most important lessons.

As we trace the activities of the Israelites, we learn some important truths to help us in our own walk of faith.

## 1. Expect trials to come (Ex. 15:22–16:3)
"Let us be as watchful after the victory as before the battle," wrote saintly Andrew Bonar. It's possible to win the battle and yet lose the victory, which is what the Jews did as they left the Red Sea and began to march toward Mt. Sinai. They forgot that life is a pilgrimage during which we must learn

new lessons and fight new battles. One great victory doesn't settle everything; we need challenging new experiences that will help us mature and glorify God. Yes, life is a school, and the Lord knows just when to give us an examination.[1]

*"What shall we drink?" (Ex. 15:22-27)* Uppermost in the minds of the Israelites wasn't how to please God but "What shall we eat?" and "What shall we drink?" According to Jesus, these questions reveal an anxious heart, not a trusting heart (Matt. 6:21, 25-33), and this can lead to all kinds of problems.

A single day in the wilderness without water would be tolerable, two days would be difficult, but three days would be impossible, especially for the children and animals. And then to be disappointed by finding bitter water would only make the situation worse. (The word "Marah" means "bitter" and is related to the word "myrrh.") But God was testing His people, not because He didn't know their hearts, but because they didn't know their own hearts. People often say, "Well, I know my own heart," but they forget that "the heart is deceitful above all things, and desperately wicked; who can know it?" (Jer. 17:9)

The Lord tests us to encourage spiritual growth and bring out the best in us, but the devil tempts us to bring out the worst in us and to encourage spiritual immaturity. The attitude that we take toward our difficulties determines which direction life will go, for what life does to us depends on what life finds in us. If we trust God and obey His Word, we'll pass the test and grow; but if in unbelief we complain and disobey the Lord, we'll fail the test and remain immature (James 1:12-18; Heb. 12:1-11).

The people of Israel were experts when it came to murmuring and complaining (Ex. 16:1-12; Num. 14:2, 27-29; 16:41; 17:1-10; Deut. 1:27; Pss. 78:17ff; 106:14). While God was testing them, they were tempting Him by their attitude and their words. To tempt God means to deliberately adopt a disobedient posture and dare Him to do anything about it. On more than one occasion in their wilderness wanderings, the Israelites invited the judgment of God by their obstinate attitude and their persistent grumbling. Our Heavenly Father is long-suffering and gracious, but sometimes He has to "spank" His children to teach us how to behave.

Complaining doesn't solve problems, and if we try to run away from a difficult situation ("Back to Egypt!"), we'll meet the same problems in the new place and still have to solve them. Of course, the heart of every problem is the problem in the heart, and the hearts of many of the Jews were not right with God. They remembered the food they ate in Egypt but forgot the wonders God had performed (Ps. 106:7), and some of them had begun to worship the gods of Egypt that Jehovah had humiliated and judged (Josh. 24:14; Ezek. 20:6-9; 23:8). Imagine worshiping idols and then complaining to God about your problems!

Moses took the right approach, the way of faith: he cried out to the Lord and then followed God's orders. God can solve our problems by changing things (like making the bitter waters sweet), by giving us something else (like the wells of water at Elim), or by giving us the grace we need to bear with our difficulties and not complain. The third approach is what produces lasting spiritual growth (2 Cor. 12:7-10).

To make "the tree" a picture of the cross of Christ is to go beyond what this passage teaches. Certainly God's children find victory in their trials by identifying with Christ in His death (Rom. 6) and resurrection (Rom. 8), but that isn't the lesson of this passage. The emphasis is on trusting God and obeying Him, knowing that the will of God will never lead us where the grace of God can't keep us. When we experience trials, our complaining is evidence of unbelief, but our obedience is evidence of faith.

From this difficult experience, the Jews not only learned something about themselves and about life, but they also learned something about their God, that He is "Jehovah Ropha, the Lord who heals" (Ex. 15:26).[2] God promised Israel abundant physical blessings if they would obey Him, but physical afflictions if they disobeyed (Deut. 7:12-15; 28). These promises were a part of the Old Covenant with Israel and aren't repeated in the New Covenant for believers today. If it is His will, God is certainly able to heal every disease *except the last one,* but our attitude must always be, "Not my will but Thy will be done."

If life were nothing but tests, we would be discouraged. If life were all pleasure, we would never learn discipline and develop character. The Lord knows how to balance the experiences of life, for He brought His people to Elim where they found plenty of water and opportunity for rest. Let's be grateful that the Lord gives us enough blessings to encourage us and enough burdens to humble us, and that He knows how much we can take.

*"What shall we eat?" (Ex. 16:1-3)* The Wilderness of Sin lay on the eastern shore of the Red Sea and must not be confused with the Wilderness of Zin which lay south of Palestine and east of Edom (Num. 13:21; 33:11-12). The word "Sin" should not be interpreted in its English meaning, as though Israel were traveling through a "sinful" place. The word "Sin" is related to "Sinai" but the meaning is uncertain.

The whole congregation complained because they were hungry. They had been away from Egypt only a month and still remembered the "flesh pots" of Egypt and the food they had eaten "to the full." But for some reason, they'd forgotten the bondage, the beatings, and the misery of their forced labor as slaves. They accused Moses and Aaron of deliberately leading them into the wilderness to kill them. They said they wished the Lord had killed them in Egypt when they

THE SCHOOL OF LIFE

were full rather than in the desert when they were empty! Little did these Israelites know that they would one day get their request, for the entire older generation would die in the wilderness and never get to the Promised Land.

## 2. Trust God to supply the need (Ex. 16:4-18)

God heard their murmurings and in His grace and mercy met their needs. He told them that in the evening, they would have flesh to eat (v. 8), and in the morning He would rain bread from heaven (v. 4). By giving them these special provisions, He was also testing them to see if they would believe and obey.

*God's promise (Ex. 16:4-5, 8, 11-12)*. In our pilgrim journey through life, we live on *promises* and not *explanations*. When we hurt, it's a normal response to ask "Why?" but that is the wrong approach to take. For one thing, when we ask God that question, we're assuming a superior posture and giving the impression that we're in charge and God is accountable to us. God is sovereign and doesn't have to explain anything to us unless He wants to. Asking "Why?" also assumes that if God did explain His plans and purposes to us, we'd understand everything perfectly and feel better.

As you read the Book of Job, you see Job frustrated with God and repeatedly saying, "I'd like to meet God and ask Him a few things!" But when God finally comes to Job, *Job is so overwhelmed he doesn't ask God a thing!* (See Job 40:1-5.) Can we begin to understand the ways and plans of God when His ways are far above us and His wisdom unsearchable? (Isa. 55:8-9; Rom. 11:33-36) Explanations don't heal broken hearts, but promises do, because promises depend on faith, and faith puts us in contact with the grace of God.

*God's glory (Ex. 16:6-7, 9-10)*. The important thing was that Israel focus on the glory of God and not on their own appetites. If they walked by faith, they would glorify the Lord and bring honor to His name. It isn't important that we're comfortable in life, but it is important that God is glorified.

When circumstances are difficult, we're prone to pray, "Lord, *how* can I get out of this?" when we ought to be praying, "Lord, *what* can I get out of this?" It isn't important that we get our way, but it is important that God accomplishes His purposes and receives all the glory (Matt. 6:33). God permits trials so that He can build godly character into His children and make us more like Jesus. Godliness isn't the automatic result of reading books and attending meetings; it also involves bearing burdens, fighting battles, and feeling pain.

*God's faithfulness (Ex. 16:13-15).* That evening, the quail flew over the camp of Israel and the people caught them, dressed them, and cooked them. They had asked for fresh meat, and God provided it. The Jews had seen wild fowl before, but what happened the next morning was altogether new, for the manna appeared on the dew on the ground. God prepared a table in the wilderness and shared "the bread of angels" with His people (Ps. 78:17-25).

The word "manna" comes from the question the Jews asked that first morning: "What is it?" (In Hebrew, *man hu.*) Manna was to be their food for the next forty years, until the new generation entered the Promised Land and the manna ceased (Ex. 16:35; Josh. 5:11-12). Each morning the Jews participated in a miracle as they emerged from their tents to find all the nourishment they needed waiting on the dew. The manna was small, like a seed, but it tasted sweet like honey (Ex. 16:31).

*God's Son (John 6:22-59).* The day after He fed more than 5,000 people with five barley loaves and two small fish, Jesus preached a sermon about "the bread of life" to a crowd in the synagogue in Capernaum. They wanted Him to prove He was the Messiah by duplicating the miracle of the manna (vv.

30-31), but instead, He declared that He was "the true bread" that came down from heaven. The Old Testament manna was a type[3] or picture of God's Son who came to give Himself as the Bread of Life for hungry sinners.

The Jews in the synagogue were following Jesus mainly because He gave them food for the body, but what they needed even more was food for the soul (Isa. 55:2). Jesus is the Bread of Life, and the only way to be saved is to receive Him into our inner being just as the body receives food. God gave the manna only to Israel, but He sent Jesus for the whole world. The manna only *sustained* their physical life in the wilderness, but God's Son *gives* eternal life to the whole world. Just as the Jews had to stoop and pick up the manna, and then eat it, so sinners must humble themselves and receive Jesus Christ within. The Jews ate the manna and eventually died, but whoever receives Jesus Christ will live forever.

There's a second application to the miracle of the manna: each day, you and I must "feed on Jesus Christ" by reading the Word, meditating on it, and obeying what it says. The Jews in the synagogue thought that Jesus was speaking about literally eating His flesh and blood (John 6:52-56), something that was contrary to Jewish law.[4] Jesus made it clear that He was speaking in spiritual language and referring to receiving His Word (vv. 61-63). However, Peter got the message (vv. 67-68), and so must we. God's Word is the heavenly food that nourishes our spiritual life, and we must feed on it daily (Job 23:12; Jer. 15:16; Matt. 4:4; 1 Peter 2:2; Heb. 5:12-14).

### 3. Obey God's instructions (Ex. 16:16-31)

Since God is not the author of confusion (1 Cor. 14:33), whenever He starts something new, He always gives the instructions necessary to make the venture successful. If we obey His instructions, He will bless, but if we disobey, there will be disappointment and discipline. The principle is still, "Let all things be done decently and in order" (1 Cor. 14:40).

*The gathering of the manna (Ex. 16:18, 21).* To begin with, the Jews were instructed to gather their manna daily, but only as much as each person in the family could eat (v. 16). An omer was a Hebrew dry measure equivalent to about two quarts. The manna was especially nutritious because eating it sustained an adult for a day's march in the wilderness. It appears that the members of each family pooled their supply each day and never lacked for sufficient food.[5] Since the Jews marched and camped by tribes (Num. 1–2), no doubt each clan and family pooled the manna they'd gathered and saw to it that everybody was adequately fed.

It was important that the Jews got up early to gather the manna, because the hot desert sun would melt it (Ex. 16:21). There was no place in the camp of Israel for the sluggard who stayed in bed while others gathered his food. There's a lesson here for believers today: we must start the day with the Lord, gathering spiritual food from the Word, because if we wait too long to meet God, the day will become cluttered, we'll get distracted, and we'll suffer from spiritual malnutrition. The "early risers" of the Bible include Abraham (Gen. 19:27; 21:14; 22:3), Jacob (28:18), Moses (Ex. 8:20; 9:13; 24:4), Joshua (Josh. 3:1, 6), Samuel (1 Sam. 15:12), Job (Job 1:5), David (Pss. 57:8; 108:2), and our Lord Jesus Christ (Mark 1:35).

*The keeping of the manna (Ex. 16:19-21).* Lazy Israelites might plan to save some manna so they could sleep in the next morning, but Moses warned them not to do so. Some of the Jews did it anyway, and their manna soured, smelled, bred maggots, and had to be thrown away. Not only were these people disobedient to God's instructions, but they were living contrary to God's own practice, for the Lord arranged for the sun to melt the manna that still lay on the ground. It doesn't pay to rebel against what God says in His Word and the example He sets in His creation.

Again, there's a personal warning here for God's people today: We can't hoard His Word and try to live on yesterday's spiritual nourishment. It's good to hear the Bible preached and taught on the Lord's Day, but we need fresh manna each day if we want to be healthy Christians. There's no substitute for a daily time alone with God, gathering fresh nourishment from His Word.

*Manna for the Sabbath (Ex. 16:22-31).* In verse 23, the Sabbath is mentioned by name for the first time in Scripture. It's called "the seventh day" in Genesis 2:1-3 and commemorated the Lord's rest after six days of creation. It seems obvious that the Jews were taught to observe the Sabbath even before God gave Moses the Ten Commandments.

While many sincere people call Sunday the Sabbath, this isn't biblical, for the Sabbath is the seventh day and Sunday is the first day of the week. The Sabbath was a day given especially by the Lord to the Jewish people as a reminder of His covenant with them (Ex. 20:8-11; 31:12-17; Neh. 9:13-15). The word "sabbath" in Hebrew means "to cease working, to rest" and is related to the Hebrew word for "seven."

So they didn't have to work on the Sabbath, the Jews were supposed to prepare their meals in advance, and this included the gathering of the manna. They were permitted on the sixth day to gather twice as much manna, and whatever they saved up would not become rancid. Not only was the giving of the manna a miracle six days a week, but the preserving of the manna for the seventh day was an additional miracle. There are always some people who don't really get the message. Some of the Jews went out on the Sabbath, looking for manna, and they found none. They didn't obey Moses' instructions! Remember, the gathering of the manna was a test from God to see if His people would obey the Law He was about to give them (Ex. 16:4). If they wouldn't obey a simple thing like gathering manna six days a week, how would they ever obey the statutes and laws that Moses would bring down from Mt. Sinai! It was a privilege to eat "the bread of angels," sent from heaven; and it was an insult to the Lord to disobey the instructions He had given.

**4. Remember the lessons God teaches you (Ex. 16:32-36)**
The instructions in verses 33-34 anticipate the giving of the Law (or "testimony"; 31:18; 32:15) and the making of the ark of testimony (25:16, 22; 26:33) and the construction of the tabernacle. The information in 16:35 was added years later to complete the account. At that time, Moses wouldn't have known how many years Israel would march in the wilderness.

As we shall see later, the ark of the testimony was the throne of God in the camp. It stood in the holy of holies in the tabernacle, where the glory of God dwelt; and within the ark were the two tablets of the law, Aaron's rod, and the golden jar of manna (Heb. 9:4). Only the high priest could enter the holy of holies, and that only once a year, but the Jewish people knew what was in the ark and taught this truth to their children. Each of these items reminded the nation of an important truth: that He is King and Lawgiver; that He established the priesthood; and that He fed His people because He cared for them.

God gave the Law to Israel because He loved His people. They needed a light to guide them, and God's Law is a lamp and a light; and obeying the Law means life (Prov. 6:23). When the people disobeyed, they needed a priest to help them be forgiven and reconciled to God. They also needed to be reminded that it was God who provided food for them, and that they didn't live by bread alone but by the Word of

God (Deut. 8:1-3).

Most people are prone to forget the way God has dealt with them, and they have to learn again the lessons they've forgotten. Some keep a journal and review it regularly, while others keep a "spiritual diary" in the margins of their Bible, noting special verses and experiences related to them. A photograph that may mean little to us conveys treasures of spiritual truth to the owner who knows why the photo is on the shelf. However we do it, we need to "nail down" the important lessons of life and permit them to influence us to walk with God and obey Him.

When by faith we walk with the Lord, then life is a school; and the successful pilgrim/students pray with Moses: "So teach us to number our days, that we may apply our hearts unto wisdom" (Ps. 90:12).

Are you among them?

# S E V E N

## *"The Lord of Hosts Is with Us"*

On April 18, 1874 the body of missionary/explorer David Livingstone was laid to rest in a grave in the center of the nave in Westminster Abbey. During the funeral service, the congregation sang a hymn by Philip Doddridge and John Logan that's based on Genesis 28:20-21.

> O God of Bethel, by whose hand
> Thy people still are fed;
> Who through this earthly pilgrimage
> Hast all our fathers led:
> Through each perplexing path of life
> Our wandering footsteps guide;
> Give us each day our daily bread,
> And raiment fit provide.

During his difficult and demanding years in Africa, Livingstone rested his faith and his future on the parting words of Jesus, "Lo, I am with you alway, even unto the end of the world" (Matt. 28:20). Concerning this verse, Livingstone had written in his journal on January 14, 1856: "It is the word of a gentleman of the most strict and sacred honor, so there's an end of it!" He knew that his Lord's word could be trusted!

It was the presence of the Lord that gave Moses the strength and confidence he needed as he led the people of

Israel during their wilderness wandering. He had a difficult task, leading a thankless army of former slaves whom he was trying to build into a nation, but he persevered because the Lord was with him. The events recorded in these two chapters reveal to us what the presence of the Lord means to God's people and their leaders as they are on their pilgrim journey.

## 1. God directs our steps (Ex. 17:1-7)

As they moved toward Mt. Sinai, the people of Israel were still being led by the pillar of cloud by day and the pillar of fire by night. But the Lord was still directing Israel into difficult and trying situations in order to prove His power and build their faith and character. After all, life's journey involves much more than merely reaching a destination. If we aren't growing in faith, in the knowledge of God, and in godly character, we're wasting our opportunities.

*An old test repeated (Ex. 17:1-3).* Israel had a long way to go before they would qualify as a godly nation. So far, every new trial they experienced only brought out the worst in them. When they arrived in Rephidim, in the Wilderness of Sinai, they again found themselves without water. They had failed this test once before, so God had to test them again. He had proved that He was able to provide water and food for them, so why were they quarreling with Moses? *Because their hearts were still in Egypt!* They were guilty of ingratitude and unbelief, wanting to go back to the old life; and as a result, they again failed to pass the test.

Every difficulty God permits us to encounter will become either a test that can make us better or a temptation that can make us worse, and *it's our own attitude that determines which it will be.* If in unbelief we start complaining and blaming God, then temptation will trap us and rob us of an opportunity to grow spiritually. But if we trust God and let Him have His way, the trial will work for us and not against us (Rom. 8:28; James 1:12-15) and help us grow in grace.

When people are out of fellowship with the Lord, and are angry and bitter, they usually want to do unreasonable things that could only make the situation worse. In this instance, the people wanted to stone their leader! (Ex. 17:5) How that would have changed their situation is difficult to discern, but disobedient people often look for a scapegoat.[1]

*An unfailing resource (Ex. 17:4-7).* Moses did what he frequently had to do as a leader: he called on the Lord for help (15:25; 32:30ff; Num. 11:1-2; 12:13; 14:13ff). "God is our refuge and strength, a very present help in trouble" (Ps. 46:1). The Lord instructed him to take some of the elders with him, plus the rod that symbolized God's power (Ex. 7:20), and to smite the rock in the sight of the people. When Moses obeyed, the water gushed forth from the rock and met the needs of the people and the livestock (Pss. 78:15-16; 105:41; 114:8; Isa. 48:21). A gracious God met the needs of a complaining people.[2]

The rock is a type of Jesus Christ smitten for us on the cross (1 Cor. 10:4),[3] and the water is a type of the Holy Spirit whose coming was made possible by Christ's death, resurrection, and ascension to heaven (John 7:37-39). This explains why Moses was wrong to smite the rock when he should have spoken to it (Num. 20:1-13), because "[Christ] died to sin once for all" (Rom. 6:10, NKJV, and see Heb. 7:27; 9:26-28).

"Massah" means "to test," and "Meribah" means "contention, quarreling." The Jews had not yet learned that *God tests His people in the everyday experiences of life.* He uses the difficult experiences of life to strengthen our faith and mature our character. But Israel's faith in God was very weak, for they thought their God had led them to a place where He couldn't care for them! The trouble with the

Israelites was that they had hard hearts that wouldn't submit to the Lord, so they rebelled against His will. In fact, the older generation had unbelieving hearts throughout their entire journey from Egypt to Canaan (Ps. 95:6-11; Heb. 3).[4] They complained about water at the beginning of their pilgrimage and also forty years later at the end (Num. 20:1-13).

On the map of our lives, how many places ought to be named "Testing and Quarreling" because of the way we've complained about our circumstances and failed to trust God? It's one thing to sit comfortably in church and sing "All the way my Savior leads me, what have I to ask beside?" and quite something else to  be confronted with distress and disappointment and meekly say, "Not my will but Thine be done." Corrie ten Boom used to say, "Don't bother to give God instructions; just report for duty."

## 2. God defeats our enemies (Ex. 17:8-16)

On the journey of faith, we not only experience trials involving the necessities of life, such as bread and water, but we also face battles when our enemies attack us. We're pilgrims who are also soldiers, and that means we must occasionally endure hardship as we follow the Lord (2 Tim. 2:3-4).

*The enemy (Ex. 17:8).* The devil is our greatest enemy (1 Peter 5:8), and he uses the world and the flesh to oppose us (Eph. 2:1-3). Just as Israel was delivered from Egypt by the power of God, so God's people today have been delivered from "this present evil world [age]" (Gal. 1:3-4) through the victory of Christ. We are *in* the world physically but not *of* the world spiritually (John 17:14-16), and therefore must not become conformed to the world (Rom. 12:2). We renounce the things of the flesh (Gal. 5:16-21) and resist the attacks of the devil (James 4:7; 1 Peter 5:8-9).

The Amalekites were the descendants of Jacob's brother Esau (Gen. 36:12, 16) who was "a profane person" (Heb.

12:16). The word translated "profane" ("godless," NIV) comes from a Greek word that means "a threshold"; it refers to somebody who is accessible and can be "walked on" by anybody or anything. The English word "profane" comes from the Latin and means "outside the temple," that is, unhallowed and common. Esau lived for the world and the flesh and despised spiritual things (v. 17). Esau opposed his brother Jacob and threatened to kill him (Gen. 27:41), and Esau's descendants opposed the children of Jacob (Israel) and threatened to annihilate them.

There's no record that the Jews ever had to fight any battles in Egypt, but once they were delivered from bondage, they discovered they had enemies. So it is in the Christian life. When we identify with Jesus Christ, then His enemies become our enemies (Luke 12:49-53) and we must "fight the good fight of faith" (1 Tim. 6:12). But we need the battles of life to help balance the blessings of life; otherwise, we'll become too confident and comfortable and stop trusting the Lord.

*The strategy (Deut. 25:17-19).* The Amalekites attacked Israel suddenly from behind, at the weakest place in the camp, for they struck those Jews who were weary and feeble and were at the rear of the march. Amalek attacked after Israel had experienced a great blessing in the provision of the water from the rock. Satan and his demonic army (Eph. 6:10-12) know what our weakest point is and when we're not ready for an assault. That's why we must "watch and pray, lest [we] enter into temptation. The spirit truly is ready, but the flesh is weak" (Mark 14:38, NKJV).

The enemy often attacks God's people after they've experienced special blessings, but the Lord can use those attacks to keep us from trusting the gifts instead of the Giver. It was after his victory over the four kings that Abraham was tempted to take the spoil (Gen. 14:17-24); and after the victory over

Jericho, Joshua became overconfident and was defeated at Ai (Josh. 7). After Elijah defeated the priests of Baal, he became discouraged and was tempted to quit (1 Kings 18:41–19:18); and it was after the blessings at His baptism that our Lord was led into the wilderness to be tempted (Matt. 3:13–4:1). "Therefore let him who thinks he stands take heed lest he fall" (1 Cor. 10:12).

*The victory (Ex. 17:9-13)*. There's no evidence that Israel fought any battles in Egypt. Even on the night of their deliverance from Egypt, they didn't have to fight the attacking Egyptian army, because the Lord fought for them. "Stand still, and see the salvation of the Lord which He will show to you today" (Ex. 14:13). But now that they were on their pilgrim journey, Israel would have to enter into battle many times and trust the Lord for victory. "And this is the victory that overcomes the world, even our faith" (1 John 5:4).

This is the first mention of Joshua in the Bible, but he will be named 200 more times before Scripture ends.[5] He was born in Egypt and named Hoshea, which means "salvation." Later, Moses changed his name to "Joshua—Jehovah is salvation" (Num. 13:8, 16), which is the Hebrew equivalent of "Jesus" (Matt. 1:21; Heb. 4:8). He knew the rigors of Egyptian slavery and must have had an aptitude for military leadership for Moses to make him general of the army. He became Moses' servant (Ex. 24:13; 33:11; Josh. 1:1), for God's policy is that we first prove ourselves as faithful servants before we can be promoted to being leaders (Matt. 25:21, 23). Joshua had only one day to rally his army and get them ready for the attack, but he did it.

Israel's great victory over Amalek involved three elements: the power of God in heaven, the skill of Joshua and the army on the battlefield, and the intercession of Moses, Aaron, and Hur[6] on the top of the hill. God could have sent angels to annihilate the enemy (Isa. 37:38), but He deigns to use human instruments to accomplish His purposes. Joshua and his army would trust God and fight, Moses and his associates would trust God and intercede, and God would do the rest. In this way, God's people would grow in faith and God's name would be glorified.

It was customary for the Jews to lift up their hands when they prayed (Pss. 28:2; 44:20; 63:4; 134:2; 1 Kings 8:22, 38, 54; 1 Tim. 2:8), and since Moses held the staff of God in his hands, he was confessing total dependence on the authority and power of Jehovah. It wasn't Moses who was empowering Joshua and his army; it was the God of Abraham, Isaac, and Jacob, "the Lord of Hosts." As long as Moses held the rod up in his hands, Israel prevailed; but when he brought his hands down, Amalek prevailed.

We can understand how Joshua and the army would grow weary fighting the battle, but why would Moses get weary holding up the rod of God? To the very day of his death, he didn't lose his natural strength (Deut. 34:7), so the cause wasn't physical. *True intercession is a demanding activity.* To focus your attention on God and "pray without ceasing" (1 Thes. 5:17) can weary you as much as strenuous work. Like Epaphras, we must be "always laboring fervently" in our prayers (Col. 4:12)[7] and not just casually mentioning our requests to the Lord. Samuel M. Zwemer, missionary to the Muslim world, used to call prayer "the gymnasium of the soul," and John Bunyan wrote, "In prayer it is better to have a heart without words than words without heart." To put your full heart into intercessory prayer will cost you, but it will also bless you.

Joshua couldn't have succeeded without Moses, but Moses couldn't have prevailed without the support of Aaron and Hur. Not everybody can be a Moses or Joshua, a D.L. Moody or Billy Graham, but all Christians can be like Aaron and Hur and help hold their hands as they obey God. God is looking for people who will share in the battle and the victory because they continue steadfastly in prayer (Rom. 12:12; Isa. 59:16).

There's also a reminder here that our Savior ever lives in heaven to make intercession for us as we fight the battles of life, and His strength never fails (Heb. 7:25). Furthermore, the Holy Spirit within also intercedes for us and guides us in our praying (Rom. 8:26-27). God promises victory to those who will pray and wield the sword of the Spirit (Eph. 6:17-18).

*The testimony (Ex. 17:14-16).* Moses didn't build a monument to himself or to Joshua, or even to the victorious army of Israel. Instead, he was careful to give all the glory to God for Israel's victory by building an altar and naming it "The Lord is my Banner." In Egypt, he had probably seen the various divisions of the army, each identified with one of their many gods, so he lifted a banner to honor the only true God. Moses also gave the reason for this memorial: "For hands were lifted up to the throne of the Lord" (v. 16, NIV), referring to Moses' intercession on the hill.[8] God had answered prayer and helped His people, and Moses wanted to praise His name.

But Moses also put an entry into the official book of records[9] that Israel should contend with Amalek until that nation was completely destroyed. Israel fought them again at Kadesh-Barnea but was defeated (Num. 14:45); Gideon conquered them along with the Midianites (Jud. 6:33). King Saul failed to obey God and exterminate the Amalekites, so he lost his crown (1 Sam. 15) and was himself killed by an Amalekite (2 Sam. 1:1-16). David defeated the Amalekites who raided his camp (1 Sam. 30), and when he became king, finally subdued them (2 Sam. 8:11-12). During the reign of Hezekiah, his armies annihilated the few Amalekites who still remained. God's judgment of the Amalekites teaches us that you can't attack the throne of God and get away with it.

### 3. God deserves our praise (Ex. 18:1-12)

After reading about the trials, complaints, and battles of the Israelites, it's a relief to move into a chapter that describes the camp of Israel as a quiet place of family fellowship and daily business. Life isn't always hunger and thirst and warfare, although those are often the things we usually remember. Charles Spurgeon said that God's people are prone to engrave their trials in marble and write their blessings in the sand, and perhaps he was right.

But the best thing about this paragraph is that everybody is praising the Lord for all He did for His people. Praising God is much better than complaining to God; in fact, praise is a good antidote for a complaining spirit. "There is a great deal more said in the Bible about praise than prayer," said evangelist D.L. Moody, "yet how few praise-meetings there are!"

*Jethro's message (Ex. 18:1-6).* We met Moses' father-in-law in 2:11-22, but his presence here raises two important questions: (1) How did Jethro hear about the wonderful works of God in Egypt? and (2) When did Moses' wife and two sons return home?

It's possible that Moses sent his family back to Midian before the Lord declared war on Egypt. Then, after the Exodus, Moses sent a messenger to Jethro asking him to bring Zipporah and the two boys and meet him at Sinai. Some students reject this scenario since Moses would certainly want his family to see the Lord's judgment of Egypt and to be a part of Israel's great deliverance. What kind of leader would want his family to be comfortable back in Midian while the people were suffering in Egypt?

If the family was with him in Egypt, then sometime after the Exodus, Moses may have sent Zipporah and their two sons back to Midian to give the good news to her family. Zipporah and her party could travel much faster than the entire nation with their children and livestock, so the family would have reached Midian before Israel arrived in the region of Sinai. Having heard the good news, Jethro then sent a message to Moses saying that he was coming to the camp with Zipporah and her sons.

*Jethro's arrival (Ex. 18:7-8).* In the East, family members and friends spend a great deal of time greeting one another when they meet (Luke 10:4), especially if they haven't seen each other for a long time (Gen. 29:9-14; 33:1-7; 45:1-15). Moses showed respect for his father-in-law by going out to meet him, but it's strange that nothing is said about Zipporah and the two sons.[10]

Hospitality is the first law of the East, and Moses invited Jethro and the rest of the visitors to join him in his tent. There he rehearsed for them again the wonderful things God had done for His people. Jethro knew some of the facts about the defeat of Egypt, but Moses gave him the details and answered his questions. It wasn't a report of what Moses had done but what the Lord had done!

*Jethro's worship (Ex. 18:9-12).* Like Melchizedek (Gen. 14:17-24), Jethro was a Gentile priest (Ex. 2:16) whose testimony indicates that he knew the true and living God. He also knew the importance of Israel in the plan of God, because he said that the Lord had punished the Egyptians because they had "treated Israel arrogantly" (Ex. 18:11, NIV).

The priesthood had not yet been officially established in Israel, so there was nothing wrong with Moses, Aaron, and the Jewish elders joining Jethro in offering sacrifices to God and then enjoying a fellowship feast. During the years Moses had lived in Midian, he had no doubt participated in many sacrificial feasts with his father-in-law. This kind of fellowship anticipated the time when Messiah would die for the sins of the whole world and make redemption available to people of all nations. "For from the rising of the sun, even to its going down, My name shall be great among the Gentiles" (Mal. 1:11, NKJV).

## 4. God distributes our burdens (Ex. 18:13-27)

Moses could have taken a week off and enjoyed his family and entertained his father-in-law, but being a faithful shepherd, he was back the next day helping his people with their problems.

*The task (Ex.18:13-16).* The nation already had elders (v. 13; 4:29), but they weren't assisting Moses in the day-by-day affairs of the camp, or if they were, there were matters they couldn't settle that had to go to Moses. There were basic regulations for the management of the camp (Ex.18:16), since 2 million people couldn't very well live together and travel together without obeying some kind of code. The phrase "statutes and laws" in verse 16 can refer to the will of God in general as well as to specific ordinances from the Lord. Long before the Law was given, God blessed Abraham for obeying His commandments, statutes, and laws (Gen. 26:5).

Judicial codes are necessary for order and security in society, but they always have to be interpreted, even if they come from the Lord. Later, the priests would assist in this task (Mal. 2:4-7); but the priesthood hadn't yet been established. From the time of Ezra (Ezra 7:10), the scribes became the students and interpreters of the Law.

*The danger (Ex. 18:17-18).* Jethro knew that Moses' leadership was crucial for the future success of Israel and that any activity that drained his energy or wasted his time was bound to hurt the nation. Also, he didn't want his son-in-law to wear himself out and leave Zipporah a widow and his two grandsons without a father. No one man could minister personally to 2 million people and last very long. Even after the new arrangement had been established, Moses had to confess that the work was too much for him (Num. 11:14), so what must the burden have been like under the old system? The Hebrew word translated "easier" in Exodus 18:22 means "to take cargo from a ship." ("That will make your load lighter," NIV.)

*The suggestion (Ex.18:19-27).* Jethro's suggestion was a good one. Moses should organize the camp so that every 10 people had somebody to talk to about their civil problems. If a ruler of 10 couldn't solve the problem, it could be referred to the ruler of 50, then 100, and then 1,000.[11] After that, it would be referred to Moses himself. D.L. Moody may have had this in mind when he said, "I would rather put 10 men to work than do the work of 10 men."

A system such as this would separate the simple problems from the more complex matters so that Moses wouldn't be wasting his time on trivial matters. (If the people of Israel were anything like people today, everybody thought his or her problem was the most important!) The arrangement would also test the seriousness of the people, for not all of them would be willing to let the ruler "take their case to a higher court."

But Jethro wasn't advising Moses to "pass the buck." No, Moses was to teach the people the regulations, no doubt assisted by the chosen rulers, so they could make wise decisions. He was also to represent the people before God, which probably meant praying for them and seeking God's direction in the difficult cases. Moses was God's chosen leader, and nobody could take his place until his work was done, but he didn't have to do all the work alone.

There are those who say that Jethro was a meddler and should have minded his own business, because God could have enabled Moses to get the job done each day. "If the

Lord had wanted Moses to have help," they argue, "He would have told Moses personally." But Jethro didn't *command* Moses to follow his orders. He urged Moses to talk to the Lord about the problem and obey whatever God said (v. 23). Since Moses did adopt his father-in-law's suggestion, he must have consulted the Lord and gotten God's approval.

Moses didn't ask Jethro how to build the tabernacle or how to offer the sacrifices, because those matters were revealed to him from the Lord. But in matters of organization and management, God's people can learn from outsiders, for "the children of this world are in their generation wiser than the children of light" (Luke 16:8). Of course, we never adopt a practice or policy until we understand the principle behind it and make sure it's in agreement with Scripture (James 3:13-18).

The important thing about delegating responsibilities is that you have leaders who have ability and character, "able men, such as fear God, men of truth, hating covetousness" (Ex.18:21).[12] These qualifications remind us of the experience of the early church in finding people to assist the apostles and relieve them of lesser duties (Acts 6:1-7). These assistants had to have good reputations, be full of the Spirit and wisdom, and approved by the people.

According to Deuteronomy 1:9-18, Moses shared Jethro's counsel with the people, admitted his own weakness and weariness, and asked them to select leaders to assist him. They approved of the plan and selected the officers whom Moses then charged with the responsibilities of their offices. When Israel moved into the Promised Land, they appointed officers in each town to assist in the settling of cases (Ex. 16:18-20). God is a God of order, and He wanted all of His people to enjoy security and justice in the camp and in the land.

Whenever ministry and structure collide, and ministry is

being hindered, God's people must adjust the structure so ministry can grow. When the Jerusalem church gave the apostles the help they needed, the work expanded and many people were converted (Acts 6:7). In this rapidly changing world, Christian ministries must be flexible if they are to solve their problems and seize their opportunities. The emphasis in the Bible isn't on organization as such but on the kind of organization that involves qualified people who get the job done. Self-defeating organizations embalm their structure and refuse to change. The ministries that God blesses are open to change, so long as the principles of God's Word are obeyed.

# EIGHT

## *Hear the Voice of God*

When God spoke to Moses at the burning bush, He gave him an encouraging promise: "When you have brought the people out of Egypt, you shall serve God on this mountain" (3:12, NKJV). That promise had now been fulfilled. The Jews were at Mt. Sinai, "the mount of God" (v. 1; 4:27; 18:5; 24:13), and would remain camped there for the next eleven months.[1] God had redeemed His people (Ex. 1–18), and was now going to claim them as His own and enter into a covenant relationship with them (Ex. 19–24), just as He promised (Ex. 6:6-7).

At least eight times,[2] Moses had asked Pharaoh's permission to lead the people into the wilderness where they could worship Jehovah, and each time, Pharaoh had refused. But now Israel would meet their God at the holy mount and worship Him. Many wonderful things occurred at Sinai that day, but the greatest was that God's people heard God's voice speaking to them personally. "Has anything so great as this ever happened, or has anything like it ever been heard of? Has any other people heard the voice of God speaking out of fire, as you have, and lived?" (Deut. 4:33; 5:23-27)

When God spoke to His people, by His grace He called them to a very special life.

## 1. A life of maturity (Ex. 19:1-4)

If freedom doesn't lead to maturity, then we end up imprisoned in a bondage worse than what we had before, a bondage from within and not from without. It's bad enough to be enslaved by an Egyptian taskmaster, but it's even worse to enslave yourself and become your own taskmaster.

Moses went up to meet God on the mountain, and what God told him he came down and shared with the people.[3] The image of maturity that God used was that of the eagle, bearing its young on its wings and teaching them the glorious freedom of flight. Moses used the same image in the song he taught Israel at the close of his life. Read carefully Deuteronomy 32:10-12. What do eagles teach us about the life of maturity?[4]

At a certain stage in the development of their young, the parent eagles break up the comfortable nest and force the eaglets to fly. The young birds may not be anxious to leave the security of the nest, but they must learn to fly if they're going to fulfill their purposes in life. The adult birds stay near the fledglings and, if they fall, carry them on their strong wings until the young birds learn how to use their wings, ride the air currents, and enjoy the abilities God gave them.

The eaglets illustrate three aspects of freedom: freedom *from* (they are out of the nest, which to us is redemption); freedom *in* (they are at home in the air, which to us is maturity), and freedom *to* (they can fulfill their purpose in life, which to us is ministry). True freedom means that we're delivered from doing the bad, we're able to do the good, and we're accomplishing God's will on the earth.

From God's point of view, Egypt was a furnace of affliction for Israel (Deut. 4:20; 1 Kings 8:51; Jer. 11:4), but the Jews often saw Egypt as a "nest" where they at least had food, shelter, and security (Ex. 16:1-3; Num. 11:1-9). God delivered them from Egypt because He had something better for them to enjoy and to do, but this meant that they had to "try their wings" and experience growing pains as they moved toward maturity.

When we're maturing in the Lord, life becomes a series of open doors that lead to more and more opportunities for responsible freedom. But if we refuse to let God mature us, life becomes a series of confining iron bars that limit us. A baby is safe and comfortable in the mother's womb, but at some point the baby must be born and enter a new and demanding world of growth and maturity. From birth to death, the "turning points" of life usher in new freedoms that bring with them new privileges and new responsibilities: walking, instead of being carried; riding a bicycle and then driving a car; working at a job and earning money; learning to use that money wisely; making friends; getting married; raising children; retiring. At each "turning point," we lose something as we gain something; and this is the way the maturing process works.

Whenever the Jews complained about God's dealings with them and yearned to go back to Egypt, they were acting like little children, so God had to discipline them. The statement I quoted earlier from George Morrison needs to be quoted again: "It took one night to take Israel out of Egypt, but forty years to take Egypt out of Israel." How long is it taking the Lord to get us to fly, or are we nestlings who don't want to be disturbed?

### 2. A life of dignity (Ex. 19:5-8)

In Egypt, the Jews were nothing but weary bodies, slaves who did their masters' bidding, but the Lord had better things planned for them. They were to be His special people, and He would use them to be a blessing to the whole world (Gen. 12:3).

*God's treasured possession (Ex. 19:5, NIV).* All the nations of the earth belong to the Lord, because He's their maker and their sustainer (9:29; Pss. 24:1; 50:12; Acts 14:15-17; 17:24-28), but He's chosen Israel to be His treasured possession (Deut. 7:6; 14:2; 26:18; Ps. 135:4; Mal. 3:17). This choice was not because of Israel's merits, because they had none (Deut. 26:5-11), but because of God's love and sovereign grace (7:6-8).

That the Jews are God's chosen people doesn't mean they're better than any other nation, only that they're different, set apart by the Lord for His special work. Romans 9:4-5 reminds us of some of the spiritual treasures God has given Israel that they might be a blessing to the whole world, for "salvation is of the Jews" (John 4:22). Because Israel has these treasures and privileges, they also have a greater responsibility to love and obey God; for "from the one who has been entrusted with much, much more will be asked" (Luke 12:48, NIV).[5]

*A kingdom of priests (Ex. 19:6).* Aaron and his sons would be consecrated later to serve as priests to the nation (Ex. 28–29), but it was God's intent that *all Israel* live as priests, manifesting His truth and sharing His blessings with the world. Israel was to be God's "showcase" to the Gentiles, proving to them that there is but one true and living God and that serving Him is the way to fullness of blessing (Isa. 42:6; 49:6). Unfortunately, instead of Israel influencing the nations to worship Jehovah, the nations influenced Israel to worship idols! The Jews adopted the religions and lifestyles of the Gentiles and so desecrated themselves, their land, and the temple that God had to chasten them severely and send them into Babylonian Captivity. The day will come, however, when Israel will see her Messiah, be cleansed of her iniquities (Zech. 12:10–13:1), and become a nation of holy priests to serve the Lord (Isa. 61:6).

*A holy nation (Ex. 19:6).* "You are to be My holy people"

(22:31), that is, a people set apart for God, a people who are different. "Be holy, for I am holy" is found at least six times in Leviticus (11:44-45; 19:2; 20:7, 26; 21:8) and is repeated twice in 1 Peter 1:15-16. In every area of life, Israel's activities were governed by the fact that they belonged to God, and that included what they ate, what they wore, who they married, how they buried their dead, and especially how they worshiped.

During the plagues in Egypt, God put a difference between them and the Egyptians (Ex. 11:7), because the Jews were not to live like the pagan Gentile nations. The Jewish priests were to set the example and also teach the people to "put a difference between holy and unholy, and between clean and unclean" (Lev. 10:10; 11:47). The priests failed to do this (Ezek. 22:26; see 42:20; 44:23; 48:14-15), and their sin helped to lead the nation into defilement and destruction (Lam. 4:13).

When Moses shared this good news with the people, they enthusiastically promised to obey everything God told them to do (Ex. 19:7-8). They may have been sincere, but God knew that their hearts were prone to do evil (Deut. 5:27-29). The fact that they repeated this vow two more times didn't change their hearts or strengthen their wills (Ex. 24:3, 7), and it wouldn't be long before Israel would succumb to the idolatry that lurked in their hearts and make a golden calf and worship it (Ex. 32).

*God's people today (1 Peter 2:5, 9).* Peter borrowed the imagery of Exodus 19:6 and called the church today "a holy priesthood . . . a chosen generation, a royal priesthood, a holy nation, His own special people, that you may proclaim the praises of Him who called you out of darkness into His marvelous light" (1 Peter 2:5, 9, NKJV). Like Israel of old, God's people today must point people to the Lord and reveal by their words and deeds how wonderful He is. We're to be "living advertisements" of the grace and power of God. Are we?

### 3. A life of sanctity (Ex. 19:9-25)

Moses had returned to the Lord on the mountain and reported the people's promise to obey His commandments. The fact that God spoke with Moses personally should have given the people confidence in their leader, but subsequent events proved differently. What a privilege it was for Israel to have a leader such as Moses, and what a tragedy that they repeatedly made life difficult for him!

The emphasis in this chapter is on the sanctity of the nation as the holy people of God, and three images stand out: the changing of their clothes, the distance set between the people and God, and the storm on Mt. Sinai.

*Changing clothes and washing (Ex. 19:10-11, 14-15).* We today are accustomed to having soap and water readily available, and extra clothes hanging in our closets, but people in Bible days didn't enjoy such luxuries. They couldn't take showers daily, and only the wealthy had stores of extra garments. That's why bathing and changing clothes often marked a new beginning, such as when God restored Adam and Eve (Gen. 3:21) or when Jacob and his family returned to Bethel (35:2). Other examples are Joseph leaving prison (41:14), healed lepers returning to society (Lev. 14:8-9), David turning back to God (2 Sam. 12:20), and King Jehoiachin being shown mercy by his captors (Jer. 52:31-34). Washing and changing clothes is the Old Testament equivalent of 1 John 1:9 and 2 Corinthians 7:1.[6]

*The distance between God and the people (Ex. 19:12-13, 20-25).* Staying away from Mt. Sinai was a matter of life or death, for the presence of God sanctified the mountain. So Moses put up barriers to keep the people at a distance. He also posted guards with authority to kill from a distance anybody who broke through the barriers, and nobody was to touch the dead body. When the trumpet sounded, then Moses ascended the mountain to meet God, but even then, God sent him back to warn the people not to get too close to Mt. Sinai.

In a dramatic way, God was teaching the people the distance between a holy God and sinful men and women, as well as the danger of presumptuously rushing into the presence of the Lord. Later, Nadab and Abihu would forget this principle, and God would kill them (Lev. 10). The structure of Old Testament worship emphasized man's sinfulness and God's "otherness": the fence around the tabernacle; the veil before the holy of holies; the fact that only the priests could minister in the tabernacle and only the high priest could enter the holy of holies, and that but once a year. The emphasis was always "Keep Your Distance!"

But the New Testament emphasizes the nearness of God, for the Son of God became flesh and came to dwell on earth (John 1:14), and His name is "Immanuel—God with us" (Matt. 1:23). By His death and resurrection, Jesus opened a new and living way into the presence of God (Heb. 10:1-25), and the New Testament banner reads: "Let us draw near!" This doesn't mean that we should get "chummy" with God and act like we're His equals, but He is our Father and He welcomes our love. See Hebrews 12:18-29.

*The storm (Ex. 19:16-19; 20:18-20).* In Scripture, a storm is often a symbol of the awesome presence and power of God (Pss. 18:1-15; 29; Hab. 3:1-16). The cloud and darkness, the thunder and lightning, and the earthquake and fire, all manifested the greatness of God (Deut. 5:22-23, 27) and produced a holy fear in the hearts of the people. Even Moses trembled with fear and admitted it! (Heb. 12:21; Deut. 9:19) God was about to teach His people His Law, and "the fear of the Lord is the beginning of knowledge" (Prov. 1:7). The Jews had also seen the plagues in Egypt, and this mighty demonstration of God's power should have also prepared their hearts to obey Him (Ps. 105:26-45).

The combination of washing themselves and changing their clothes, witnessing the storm, and keeping their distance from Sinai, couldn't help but impress the people with their own sinfulness and God's majestic holiness. They were called to be a sanctified people, unlike the nations around them. Only as they obeyed God could they truly enjoy the privileges of being a kingdom of priests, God's special treasure and His holy nation.

### 4. A life of responsibility (Ex. 20:1-17)[7]

The privilege of freedom brings with it the responsibility to use that freedom wisely for the glory of God and the good of others. However, the Ten Commandments were much more than laws for governing the life of the nation of Israel. They are part of the covenant God made with Israel when He took them to Himself to be His special people (6:1-8; 19:5-8). In the Abrahamic Covenant, God gave the Jews the title deed to the Promised Land (Gen. 12:3; 13:14-18), but Israel's possession and enjoyment of that land depended on their obedience to the Mosaic Covenant. The tragedy is that the nation disobeyed the Law, defiled their land, and grieved their Lord, so they had to be chastened.

The Law was never given as a way of salvation for either Jews or Gentiles, because "by the works of the law shall no flesh be justified" (Gal. 2:16). Salvation is not a reward for good works but the gift of God through faith in Jesus Christ (Rom. 4:5; Eph. 2:8-9). The Law reveals God's righteousness and demands righteousness, but it can't give righteousness (Gal. 2:21); only Jesus Christ can do that (2 Cor. 5:21). The Law is a mirror that reveals where you're dirty, but you don't wash your face in the mirror (James 1:22-25). Only the blood of Jesus Christ can cleanse us from sin (1 John 1:7, 9; Heb. 10:22).

God doesn't give His Spirit to us because we obey the Law (Gal. 3:2) but because we trust Christ (4:1-7), nor does He give us our inheritance through the Law (3:18). The one thing the dead sinner needs is life (Eph. 2:1-3), but the Law can't give life (Gal. 3:21). Then what's the purpose of the Law? It's God's way of showing us our sins and stripping us of our self-righteousness so that we cry out for the mercy and grace of God.[8] God gives His Holy Spirit to all who believe on His Son, and the Spirit enables us to obey God's will and therefore fulfill the righteousness of the Law (Rom. 8:1-3).[9]

One of the main ministries of the Law was to prepare the way for the birth of Christ (Gal. 4:1-7). The nation of Israel was like an immature child who needed a "guardian" to care for him, to instruct and protect him, the way slaves in Paul's day cared for their masters' children. But when children mature, the guardians aren't needed anymore. The Jewish ceremonial system presented in Exodus and Leviticus was fulfilled by Christ, but the moral content of God's Law still remains, and nine of the Ten Commandments are repeated in the New Testament epistles for the church to honor and obey. The Sabbath commandment isn't repeated, and we'll say more about that later.

While all the Ten Commandments deal with our responsibilities toward God, the first four are particularly Godward while the last six are manward. How we relate to others depends on how we relate to God; for if we love God and obey Him, we'll also love our neighbors and serve them (Matt. 22:34-40; Rom. 13).

*Recognizing one true God (Ex. 20:1-3).* The phrase "the Lord thy God" is repeated five times in this section (vv. 3, 5, 7, 10, 12) to remind the people of the authority behind these commandments. Moses isn't reporting "ten opinions" that he heard from a friendly counselor, but ten commandments spoken by Almighty God. The Jews lived in a world of blind and superstitious nations that worshiped many gods, something Israel beheld for centuries in Egypt.[10] Israel was to bear witness of the true and living God (Ps. 115) and invite their neighbors to trust Him.

The phrase "before Me" can mean "in opposition to Me." For the Jews to worship another god would be to declare war on Jehovah and incur His wrath. Each morning, the faithful Jew declares, "Hear, O Israel, the Lord our God is one Lord" (Deut. 6:4).

*Worshiping only the Lord (Ex. 20:4-6).*[11] An idol is a substitute for God and therefore not a god, for there is only one true and living God. Present-day religious pluralism ("You worship your god and I'll worship mine, because both are right") is both unbiblical and illogical, for how can there be more than one god? If God is God, He is infinite, eternal, and sovereign and can't share the throne with another being who is also infinite, eternal, and sovereign.

"I am the Lord: that is My name; and My glory I will not give to another, neither My praise to graven [carved] images" (Isa. 42:8). The idol worship of the pagan nations was not only illogical and unbiblical, but it was intensely immoral (temple prostitutes and fertility rites), inhuman (sacrificing children), and demonic (1 Cor. 10:10-22). No wonder the Lord commanded Israel to destroy the temples, altars, and idols of the pagans when they invaded the land of Canaan (Deut. 7:1-11).

"Little children, keep yourselves from idols" (1 John 5:21) was the Apostle John's final admonition to Christians in his day, and the admonition needs to be heeded today. If an idol is anything that takes the place of God, anything to which we devote our energy and time, or for which we make sacrifices because we love it and serve it, then John's warning is needed today. The idols that entice God's people today are things like money, recognition, success, material possessions (cars, houses, boats, collectibles), knowledge, or even other people.

God is a "jealous God," not in the sense that He's envious of other gods, for He knows that all other "gods" are figments of the imagination and don't really exist. The word "jealous" expresses His love for His people because He wants the very best for them. Just as parents are jealous over their children and spouses over their mates, so God is jealous over His beloved ones and will not tolerate competition (Zech. 1:14; 8:2). In Scripture, idolatry is the equivalent of prostitution and adultery (Hosea 1–3; Jer. 2–3; Ezek. 16; 23; James 4:4-5). God desires and deserves the exclusive love of His people (Ex. 34:14; Deut. 4:24; 5:9; 6:15).

God is so serious about receiving exclusive worship and love that He punishes those who refuse to obey Him. God doesn't punish the children and grandchildren for somebody else's sins (24:16; Ezek. 18:4), but the sad consequences of ancestral sins can be passed from generation to generation and innocent children suffer because of what their parents or grandparents have done. In Bible times, it wasn't unusual for four generations to live in the same extended family and thus have greater opportunity to influence and affect one another.

At the same time, the godliness of ancestors can help to bring blessing to succeeding generations. Abraham's faith brought blessing to his descendants, and David's ministry helped people long after he had died. My great-grandfather prayed that there would be a preacher of the Gospel in every generation of his family, and God has answered that prayer!

*Honoring God's name (Ex. 20:7).* Your name stands for your character and reputation, what you are and what you do (John 17:6, 26). When you say that someone has "a bad

name," you're not criticizing what's written on his birth cer-
tificate. You're warning me that the man can't be trusted. If
God is the greatest being in the universe, then His name is
the greatest name and must be honored. The first petition in
the Lord's Prayer is, "Hallowed be Thy name" (Matt. 6:9).
People blaspheme God's name by using vulgar language.
But using God's name in making a promise or taking an
oath, and then not fulfilling the commitment, is cheapening
His name and blaspheming God (Lev. 19:12).

*Honoring the Sabbath (Ex. 20:8-11).* The word "sabbath"
means "rest." The Sabbath tradition was already a part of Israel's life (16:23, 25), but now it became a part of Israel's law
and their covenant relationship with God. While the Sabbath
was rooted in creation (Gen. 2:1-3), it was also a special sign
between Israel and the Lord (Ex. 31:12-17; Neh. 9:13-15;
Ezek. 20:12, 20); and there's no biblical evidence that God
commanded any Gentile nation to observe the seventh day
(Ps. 147:19-20). Later, Moses associated the Sabbath with
Israel's deliverance from Egypt (Deut. 5:12-15), a foretaste of
the rest they would enjoy in their promised inheritance (3:20;
12:10; 25:19).

When the Jews observed the Sabbath, it was not only a
mark of their devotion to the Lord, but it was also a witness
to their pagan neighbors to whom the seventh day was just
another day. By resting on the seventh day, the Jews were
promoting their own welfare as well as that of their servants
and farm animals, acknowledging the lordship of Jehovah
over time and creation (Ex. 23:12). From earliest times,
God's people assembled on the first day of the week to honor
the resurrection of Jesus Christ (John 20:19, 26; Acts 20:7;
1 Cor. 16:2), but the principle of one day in seven still stands
(Col. 2:16-17; Gal. 4:1-11; Rom. 14:1–15:7).

It's unfortunate that the Israelites didn't honor the Sabbath as God directed and had to be disciplined (2 Chron.

36:14-21; Ezek. 20; Isa. 58:13-14; Jer. 17:19-27). It's also unfortunate that the scribes and Pharisees added thirty-nine forbidden acts to this commandment so that observing the Sabbath became a burden instead of a blessing (Mark 2:23–3:5).

*Honoring one's parents (Ex. 20:12).* In a world that worships and imitates youth and uses "assisted suicide" (euthanasia) to eliminate unwanted old people, this commandment sounds like an echo from a time warp. But the Jews were taught to respect age and to care for their senior citizens (21:15, 17; Lev. 19:3, 32; Deut. 27:16; Prov. 1:8; 16:31; 20:20; 23:22; 30:17), a good example for us to follow today (Eph. 6:1-3; 1 Tim. 5:1-2).[12] Someone has said that the elderly are the only outcast group that everybody expects to join, because nobody wants the alternative. But how we treat them today will help to determine how we're treated tomorrow, because we reap what we sow.

*Honoring human life (Ex. 20:13).* Life is a gift from God, and only He has the authority to take life. Because we're made in God's image, murder is an attack against God (Gen. 1:26-27; 9:6). Protecting life is the responsibility of every member of society, not just the public officials (Rom. 13). The issue here is premeditated murder, which Jesus said could have its beginning in anger (Matt. 5:21-26). The Jews were allowed to defend themselves (Ex. 22:2), and the Law made concessions for accidental death; but murder was a capital offense (21:12-14).

*Honoring marriage (Ex. 20:14).* So serious was adultery that it was considered a capital crime (Lev. 20:10; Deut. 22:22). The family is the basic unit of the nation, and faithfulness to the marriage contract is the foundation for the family. Adultery is robbery (1 Thes. 4:1-8), but in the end, those who commit adultery rob themselves (Prov. 6:20-35). While the Lord can forgive the sin of adultery (1 Cor. 6:9-11; John

8:1-11), like David, the adulterer and adulteress must live with the sad consequences of forgiven sin (2 Sam. 12:13-14; Ps. 51). Adultery begins with the desire in the heart caused by the second look (Matt. 5:27-30).

*Respecting personal property (Ex. 20:15).* God gave Israel an elaborate set of laws to govern their use of the land, because the land belonged to Him and they were but stewards (Lev. 25:2, 23, 38). This fact is the basis for a sane ecology. Ephesians 4:28 teaches that there are only three ways to get wealth: work for it, have it given to you, or steal it, and stealing is wrong.

*Speaking the truth (Ex. 20:16).* Speaking the truth and honoring promises is the cement that holds society together. To tell lies in court is to undermine the very law itself, which explains why Moses required the witnesses to be the executioners in capital crimes (Deut. 17:6-13). It's one thing to lie, but quite something else to kill in order to protect your lie. This commandment also prohibits slandering people (Ex. 23:1; Prov. 10:18; 12:17; 19:9; 24:28; Titus 3:1-2; James 4:11; 1 Peter 2:1).

*Controlling desires (Ex. 20:17).* The first and tenth commandments deal with what's in the heart, while the other eight focus on outward actions that begin in the heart. Covetous people will break all of God's commandments in order to satisfy their desires, because at the heart of sin is the sin in the heart (Matt. 15:19). To covet is to feed inward desires for anything that God says is sinful. It was this commandment that "slew" Saul of Tarsus and convicted this successful Pharisee that he was a sinner (Rom. 7:1-14; see Luke 12:15, Eph. 5:3, Col. 3:5).

The Ten Commandments end with an emphasis on being a good neighbor, for the second greatest commandment is to love your neighbor as yourself (Matt. 22:34-40; Lev. 19:18). If we love our neighbors, we won't covet what they have, steal from them, lie about them, or do any of the other things God prohibits in His Word. This is why love is the fulfillment of the Law (Rom. 13:8-10). But only God can change our sinful hearts (Heb. 10:14-18) and give us the love we need to obey Him and to care for others (Gal. 5:22-26; Rom. 5:1-5).[13]

EXODUS 20:22–24:8

# The Book of the Covenant

This section of Exodus includes basic laws that deal especially with the protection of human life and property. By
accepting "The Book of the Covenant" (24:3-8), the people
entered into a special relationship with Jehovah and obligated themselves to obey Him. These laws were not arbitrary;
they're based on the character of God and the unchanging
moral principles expressed in the Ten Commandments.

Law is powerless to change human nature; it can only protect life and property by regulating human behavior. One of
the most dangerous and disastrous periods in Jewish history
was the time of the judges when "every man did that which
was right in his own eyes" (Jud. 17:6; 18:1; 19:1; 21:25). The
enforcing of good laws doesn't guarantee a perfect society,
but it does promote order and prevent anarchy.

## 1. God is unseen: hear His Word (Ex. 20:22-26)

Forty years later when Moses reviewed the Law with the
new generation, he reminded them that their ancestors had
seen manifestations of God's glory and power at Sinai and
heard His words, *but they "saw no form of any kind"* (Deut.
4:15, NIV). God didn't reveal Himself in any form lest the
Jews turn the living God into a dead idol. "To whom then will
you liken God? Or what likeness will you compare to Him?"
(Isa. 40:18, NKJV)

The Jews were called to be a people of the Word. The success of the nation depended on hearing God's Word, believing it, and obeying it. The nations around Israel built their religions on what they could see—idols made by men's hands, but Israel was to worship an invisible God[1] and have nothing to do with idols. "False gods are always gods one can see (and touch)," wrote Christian philosopher Jacques Ellul, "and that very quality demonstrates their falsity and their nonexistence as gods."[2]

The Jewish scholar Abraham Joshua Heschel summarized Israel's theology of the Scriptures when he wrote, "To believe, we need God, a soul, and the Word."[3]

God warned Israel not to manufacture idols and not to build elaborate altars such as those used by the heathen nations around them (see 2 Kings 16:10-20). A simple altar of earth or unhewn stone would be acceptable to the Lord. If the stones were chiseled, they would become like idols, and the work of man would become more important than the worship of God. The natural stone provided by the Lord was all He would accept.

Both nudity and intercourse with temple prostitutes were a part of many pagan religious ceremonies, and these were expressly forbidden by the Lord. God commanded the Jewish priests to wear special garments to cover their nakedness (Ex. 28:42-43; Lev. 6:10), and if they failed to obey, they were in danger of being killed (Ex. 28:35, 43).

In spite of their enthusiastic promises, Israel quickly disobeyed these commandments. While Moses was with God on the mountain, the people made a golden calf and engaged in an idolatrous orgy that led to the death of 3,000 men (32:1-6, 25-29). Anything in religious liturgy that encourages the sensual instead of the spiritual cannot be from God or be blessed by God.

## 2. God is just: obey His laws (Ex. 21:1–23:19)

Justice is the practical outworking of the righteousness of God in human history, for "the Lord loves righteousness and justice" (Ps. 33:5; see Isa. 30:18; 61:8). There may be a great deal of injustice in our world today, but the time will come when God will judge the world in righteousness by the Savior that the world has rejected, and His judgment will be just (Acts 17:31).

*Laws about servants (Ex. 21:1-11; see also Lev. 25:39-43; Deut. 15:12-18).* Though the Jews were permitted to own slaves from other nations, usually prisoners of war, they were not allowed to enslave their own people. Two scenarios are presented here: a man who voluntarily becomes a servant (Ex. 21:1-7), and a woman who is sold to be a servant (vv. 8-11).

If because of poverty, a Jew had to become an indentured servant, his master had to treat him humanely and release him after six years of service. If because of family affection the man wanted to remain in service, and the judges approved it, then he would be marked in the earlobe and remain a servant the rest of his life. However, he was never to be treated like a slave.

A female servant wasn't automatically set free after six years. If a poor man sold his daughter to be a servant or a concubine,[4] then the girl's father would receive the sale price, the girl would get a better home, and her husband wouldn't have to pay a costly dowry. If after becoming the man's concubine she didn't please him, somebody in her birth family could redeem her and she would be set free.

If the man had chosen her for his son, and the son came to dislike her and married another woman, then the son's father had to be sure she was treated like a married daughter. That meant making sure she had clothing, food, and her conjugal rights (1 Cor. 7:1-6). If the father failed to do this, the woman was free to return to her family home and was not considered a slave.

*Capital crimes (Ex. 21:12-17).* These laws are the logical application of the sixth commandment, "Thou shalt not kill" (20:13; Lev. 24:17). We're made in God's image, so to murder a fellow human being is to attack the image of God (Gen. 9:6). If a person was found guilty of murder on the testimony of two or more witnesses (Num. 35:30-31), then the murderer was killed.

The Law made a distinction between premeditated murder and accidental manslaughter. If you killed somebody accidentally, you could flee to God's altar for safety (1 Kings 2:29) until the elders had time to study the matter. Once Israel was in their land, they set apart six cities of refuge where the manslayer could flee and be protected until the matter had been investigated (Num. 35; Deut. 19; Josh. 20). Israel didn't have a police force; the family of the victim was expected to see that justice was done. But in the heat of anger, they might be more interested in revenge than in justice, so the law stepped in to protect the accused until he was proved guilty.

*Children and parents (Ex. 21:15, 17).* Having dealt with murder in general, the law then dealt with specific cases. The first deals with a man's mistreatment of his parents, abusing them physically and/or verbally, which would be a violation of the fifth commandment (vv. 15, 17; Lev. 20:9; Deut. 27:16). It's possible that the "prodigal son law" (Deut. 21:18-21) applies here and that this son was desperately in need of discipline. Children who have no respect for their parents usually have no respect for any other authority and want only their own selfish way. "Without natural affection" (2 Tim. 3:3) describes some people in these last days, but those kind of people lived in Moses' day.

*Kidnapping is prohibited in Exodus 21:16 (Deut. 24:7).* If

it's wrong to steal property (Ex. 20:15), then it's an even greater crime to steal people made in God's image and to sell them as slaves.

*Injuries (Ex. 21:18-32).* People aren't supposed to argue to the point of blows (Prov. 15:1; 25:15), but it happens, and when it does, sometimes people are hurt. If the victim died, the aggressor would pay with his life, but if the victim convalesces and eventually is able to walk about, the aggressor is clear of further charges. However, he had to reimburse the victim for his time lost from work and for his medical expenses.

*Slaves (Ex. 21:20-21).* This principle is now applied to a master and his slaves. The Lord didn't want slaves to be looked upon as pieces of property but as humans made in God's image and deserving of their human rights. If in disciplining a slave (Prov. 10:13; 13:24), the master went too far and killed the person, the master was to be punished. We aren't told what the punishment was; it was probably determined by the judges (see Ex. 21:22) and depended on whether there was really intent to kill. (It's hard to believe that a master would want to destroy his own property and lose the income produced.) If after a few days the slave recovered, his master wasn't punished, for he had already lost income from the slave during the period of recuperation.

*A pregnant woman injured (Ex. 21:22-23).* Was she the wife of one of the combatants, and her husband was losing the fight? We don't know. Scholars don't agree on the translation of verse 22. Is it "and she gives birth prematurely" (NIV) or "and she has a miscarriage"? (NIV margin, NASB) The clause "but there is no serious injury" (either to the mother or the child) would suggest that the first translation is to be preferred, since a miscarriage would certainly be a serious thing.

Even though there was no serious injury to the mother or

the child, the court was required to fine the guilty man for his aggressive action against somebody who wasn't a party to the fight. Regardless of the man's intent, what he did could have caused the death of the child or the mother or both. But if there was serious injury, that is, the mother and/or child was maimed or killed, then the court would follow the *lex talionis* (vv. 23-25) which says, "The punishment must fit the crime."[5]

This principle has been severely criticized by some as being "barbaric," but it's just the opposite. In an age when the legal system was developing, this law made sure that the punishment meted out by the judges was equal to the seriousness and severity of the crime, not more and not less. If the guilty aggressor blinded his enemy's eye, then his own eye was blinded. Nothing could be fairer. If you broke your enemy's finger and the court ordered you to be blinded, that wouldn't be fair at all, because the sentence must fit the crime. The only time this principle was not enforced was when a master injured a slave, and the slave's compensation was his or her freedom (vv. 26-27).

When Jesus prohibited His disciples from retaliating against those who hurt them (Matt. 5:38-44; 1 Peter 2:19-21), He was dealing with personal revenge ("I'll get even with you!") and encouraging personal forgiveness. He wasn't criticizing Moses or interfering with the legal system, because He came to fulfill the Law and not to destroy it (Matt. 5:17-20). As believers, we have the privilege of waiving our "legal rights" to the glory of God and not demanding compensation (1 Cor. 6:1-8). However, a judge has to see that justice is done and the law is respected.

*Injured by an animal (Ex. 21:28-32).* The Law is clear that the owner was responsible to see that his animal didn't injure people. A dangerous bull with a record of attacking people had to be kept penned up. If he wasn't and he killed somebody, the owner was responsible, and both the owner and the animal were put to death. The animal was not eaten because it had been defiled by its awful act. However, the court could fine the owner and allow him to pay a ransom and go free (but see Num. 35:31). Note that the Law made no difference between the death of a male or a female (Ex. 21:29, 31). There was a difference, however, when it came to slaves, for the owner of the animal could pay his master thirty pieces of silver to compensate him for the loss (see Matt. 26:14-16).

*Property damage (Ex. 21:33–22:15).* In the Promised Land, Israel would become an agricultural society, and a farmer's animals were important to him, because without them he couldn't work the land.

*Animals injured or killed (Ex. 21:33-34).* If a man's carelessness and negligence caused an animal to be injured or killed, then he had to pay the owner for the animal, but the owner of the pit could claim the carcass as his own. If one animal killed another, the two owners divided both the carcass of the dead animal and the money received from the sale of the living animal. This law not only revealed God's concern for justice but also His desire that people be careful and not make it easy for animals to be injured and therefore have to be killed.

*Stealing animals (Ex. 22:1-4).* The Law made a difference between stolen animals that were killed or sold, and stolen animals still in the possession of the thief. When the thief was found guilty, in the first instance, he had to repay five to one for oxen and four to one for sheep. In the second instance, he had to restore two animals for one. It was bad enough to steal an animal, but to kill or sell that which wasn't your own was to assume rights that didn't belong to you. If he couldn't pay, he was sold as a slave and the money given to the man whose animals he stole.

This law also made a difference between the night thief and the daylight thief. In the daylight, the owner could identify the thief breaking into his pens and could even call for help from his neighbors. To kill the thief in daylight would be an unnecessary expression of revenge. But at night, the owner might not be able to identify the intruder, nor would he know if the man was armed and therefore his own life was in danger. At night it would also take longer to get help.

The law of restitution for stolen animals reminds us of David's words in 2 Samuel 12:6 and Zaccheus' promise in Luke 19:8. The Prophet Nathan saw King David as a sheep stealer and Bathsheba as the stolen lamb, for adultery is thievery (1 Thes. 4:1-7). David did repay fourfold: the baby died, Amnon and Absalom were both slain, and Tamar was raped (2 Sam. 12:15–13:33; 18:1-18).

*Crops (Ex. 22:5-6).* The boundaries of fields were marked by stones at the corners and not by fences around the tract (Deut. 19:14; 27:17; Prov. 22:28; 23:10). Grazing animals wouldn't know one field from another anyway and would wander wherever the grass was available. The owner was supposed to act like a good neighbor and keep watch. If he didn't and his animals ate in his neighbor's field, he had to make restitution in kind to his neighbor, being careful to give him the best, for restitution shouldn't be something we get away with cheaply.

During the dry season, there was always the danger of fire in the fields that could destroy the grain (Ex. 22:6). It was only right that whoever caused the fire should compensate the people who were deprived of their grain. The words "restore" and "restitution," used six times in chapter 22 (vv. 1, 3-6, 12), are a translation of the Hebrew word "shalam" that means "to make whole, to make complete" and is related to the familiar Hebrew word "shalom" ("peace, health"). It takes more than confession of guilt for an offender to make things right; it also demands effort on his part to compensate the people who were hurt. Only then can the torn fabric of relationships be mended and society be made whole.

*Other people's belongings (Ex. 22:7-15)*. Honesty and integrity form the adhesive that holds a healthy and productive society together. If neighbors can't trust each other, then life becomes difficult. If you ask me to guard your money, material things, or animals, I should faithfully do my job. In spite of my diligence, a thief may break in and steal your possessions, but when he's caught, he has to restore double. If the thief isn't caught, then I must be able to prove to the court that I wasn't careless and that I'm not the culprit. That means one of three things: presenting witnesses who can vouch for my diligence; showing pieces of the animals to prove they were killed by beasts (Gen. 31:39; Amos 3:12); or, lacking these, taking an oath of innocence before the Lord, which is a serious thing. The judges, being God's representatives to the nation, would discern whether or not I was telling the truth. If it was proved that my neighbor's animals died, strayed, or were stolen because of my negligence, then I'll have to make proper restitution.

If I borrow one of your animals for doing my farm work, and the animal is injured or dies while in my care, then I must compensate you for your loss. If you're with me at the time, guiding your own animal, I'm not obligated to pay anything. If I hired the animal from you and paid you the fee, then the fee covers the loss.

*Miscellaneous laws (Ex. 22:16–23:19)*. Most of these laws need no special explanation, but we'll note some of the truths inherent in these laws.

*Rape (vv. 16-17)*. Unmarried girls belonged to their father, and a girl who was not a virgin would not be sought as a wife, so her loss of virginity meant a loss in bridal price to her father. The offender was required to marry the girl, but if the father didn't want him as a son-in-law, the man could pay the dowry and be set free. If the girl were engaged, the rape was considered adultery, and a different law applied (Deut. 22:23-29).

*Sorcery (Ex. 22:18)*. What today is looked upon as a harmless diversion was in Moses' day rightly identified as a dangerous demonic practice. The Jews were commanded to stay away from everything that was associated with the occult (Lev. 20:6; Deut. 18:10, 14; 1 Sam. 28; Isa. 47:12-14). Galatians 5:20 associates witchcraft with idolatry.

*Bestiality (Ex. 22:19)* was also part of the religious practices of the heathen nations and was condemned by the Lord (Lev. 18:23; 20:15-16; Deut. 27:21). It was also a perversion of the wonderful gift of sex.

*Idolatry (Ex. 22:20; 23:13)*. They were not to sacrifice to other gods under penalty of death, nor were they to mention the names of these gods. Idolatry was Israel's greatest temptation during their wilderness journey and after they entered the Promised Land, and the Lord warned them to destroy the pagan temples and altars (Deut. 4:14-24).

*Selfishness (Ex. 22:21-27; 23:9)*. These laws admonish the Jews to be kind to strangers and aliens, widows and orphans, and the poor. The Jews had been strangers in Egypt and for many years were treated kindly, and widows and orphans are the special concern of the Lord (Lev. 19:9-10; Deut. 14:28-29; 16:11, 14; 24:19-21; 26:12-13; Pss. 10:14, 17-18; 68:5; 82:3; 146:9; Isa. 1:23; 10:2; Jer. 7:6; 22:3; Zech. 7:10; Mal. 3:5). The rich must not exploit the poor but give them the help they need (Lev. 25:35-38; Deut. 15:7-11; 23:19-20; 24:6, 10-13; Prov. 28:8). God hears the cries of the afflicted (Ex. 22:23, 27).

*Reviling authority (Ex. 22:28)*. They might blaspheme God with their lips but also by despising the laws He gave for their good, especially the ones relating to generosity to others (vv. 21-27). Blaspheming God was a capital offense (Lev.

24:10-16). It was against the law to speak evil of a ruler (Prov. 24:21-22; 1 Peter 2:17). Paul apologized when he inadvertently spoke evil of the high priest (Acts 23:4-5; 2 Sam. 19:19; 1 Kings 21:10). God has established human government (Rom. 13), and even if we don't respect the officer, we must respect the office.

*Delay in obeying (Ex. 22:29-30)*. The firstfruits belong to the Lord, whether it's a firstborn son, a firstborn male animal (Ex. 13), or the firstfruits of the field and orchard (Prov. 3:9-10). If it's wrong to withhold a man's garment (Ex. 22:26-27) or wages (James 5:4), how much worse is it to withhold from the Lord the gifts that He gives us to return to Him?

*Defiled meat (Ex. 22:31)*. The reason behind this law is both religious and hygienic. The bodies of animals slaughtered incorrectly would still contain blood, and the eating of blood was forbidden (Lev. 22:8). Furthermore, a carcass lying in the field could quickly become spoiled and spread disease. "Free meat" could be very expensive. A holy people wouldn't want to touch it, let alone eat it.

*Justice (Ex. 23:1-8)*. This is an amplification of the ninth commandment (20:16), a warning not to endorse falsehood and promote injustice because of what the crowd is doing (Lev. 19:15-16; Deut. 22:13-19). Nor should God's people be influenced by the wealth or the poverty of the accused or by the bribes people offer them for their support (16:18-20; Isa. 1:23; Micah 3:11). To condemn an innocent person for personal gain is to become guilty before God, and God doesn't acquit the guilty (Ex. 23:7, NIV).[6] But Moses also reminded them to be kind to their enemies and to the enemies' animals (vv. 4-5; Deut. 22:13-15). Our goodness should be the result of obeying laws but practicing love.

*Observing the feasts (Ex. 23:10-17)*. God was in charge of time and instructed the Jews to celebrate the weekly Sabbath by refraining from work. Every seven years they were to celebrate a Sabbatical Year during which the land would be allowed to rest and the poor people could avail themselves of the food that was growing without cultivation (Lev. 25:1-7). The Jews were given ecologically sound laws long ago. But this special year would be a test of their faith as well as of their obedience.

When the people were settled in their land, the men were to gather to worship three times a year, at Passover, Pentecost, and the Feast of Tabernacles. (See Lev. 23 for the Jewish religious calendar.) The men were usually accompanied by their families (see 1 Sam. 1 and Luke 2:40).

"Do not cook a young goat in its mother's milk" (Ex. 23:19, NIV; 34:26; Deut. 14:21). The young goat was a favorite food of the people, and cooking it in milk was supposed to improve the taste. To use the mother's milk to cook her own offspring would reveal an attitude of heart that could lead to all kinds of sin. Furthermore, cooking a kid this way was a part of a Canaanite pagan ceremony, and God didn't want His people emulating the idolaters. Since this law is connected with the Feast of Booths, the harvest festival, perhaps this pagan ritual had something to do with prosperity. The milk was then sprinkled on the trees and fields to help promote fertility, a magical practice that was forbidden to Israel.[7]

### 3. God is wise: follow His leading (Ex. 23:20–24:8)

The Israelites would remain at Sinai about eleven months, and then they would journey to Kadesh-Barnea where they were to enter the land (Num. 10:11–14:45). Failing to trust God and claim their inheritance, they were condemned to journey in the wilderness until the generation twenty years old and upward had all died, except for Caleb and Joshua. For thirty-eight years, God would guide His people and then bring them back to the borders of Canaan to enter and claim the land.

The angel here is Jesus Christ, the Son of God, the Angel of the Covenant (Ex. 14:19). Only He can pardon transgressions and only in Him is the wonderful name of the Lord. God had prepared a place for His earthly people (23:20) just as Jesus is preparing a place for His heavenly people (John 14:1-6). If they followed the Lord, He would meet all their needs and defeat all their enemies.

Once again, the Lord warned them about the sin of idolatry, worshiping the false gods of the nations around them, the nations that they would defeat. If Israel devoted themselves wholly to the Lord, He would go before them, confound their enemies, and enable them to conquer the land. Indeed, the "terror of God" did go before Israel and weaken the people in the land (Josh. 2:11; Ex. 15:16). The "hornet" in 23:28 could well have been the insect that we know, because the people of the East respect the hornet (Deut. 7:20; Josh. 24:12). The Hebrew word is similar to the word for Egypt (*zirah/mizraim*), so some students believe that the reference is to the Egyptian armies that frequently invaded Canaan before the Jews arrived. In Isaiah 7:18, Egypt is compared to a fly and Assyria to a bee.

It took Joshua and his army about seven years to conquer the land, and the victory was followed by a "mopping up" operation. God planned that they take the land gradually so they could control things, but some of the tribes never did fully conquer the territory that was assigned to them (Jud. 1-2). God set the boundaries of the land (Gen. 15:18-21), and they were reached during the time of David and Solomon (2 Sam. 8:1-14; 1 Kings 4:20-25), but when the nation divided, they began to lose territory to their enemies.

## 4. God is faithful: trust His covenant (Ex. 24:1-8)
The first two verses connect with 20:21, when God called Moses to ascend Sinai and bring with him the seventy

elders, Aaron, and Aaron's sons Nadab and Abihu. Moses shared the words of God with the people, and once again they promised to obey everything God told them to do (24:3; 19:8). He then wrote down all that God had said, which means the Ten Commandments and the Book of the Covenant.

But it would take more than promises to ratify the Book of the Covenant, and Moses took care of that the next morning. He built an altar to the Lord and then set up twelve pillar-like stones to represent the twelve tribes of Israel. The young men set aside to serve as priests offered sacrifices to the Lord, because it was necessary to seal the covenant with blood. Some of the blood was sprinkled on the altar, signifying that God had forgiven His people of their sins.

Moses then read the Book of the Covenant to the people and they affirmed their willingness to obey. Moses took the rest of the blood in the basins and sprinkled both the Book and the people (24:8; Heb. 9:19-20), thus ratifying the covenant. Israel had to realize their responsibility to obey the laws of the Lord. The covenant was now ratified by blood, and God would hold them to their promises. After all, they expected God to keep His promises!

The promise of the Lord in Exodus 6:6-8 was now about to move into its third phase. God had redeemed His people (Ex. 1–18) and taken them to Himself as His people (Ex. 19–24); and now He was about to come and dwell among them and be their God (Ex. 25–40). The last section of Exodus will focus on the design, construction, and dedication of the tabernacle, and it's a section rich in spiritual truth and practical lessons.

# INTERLUDE

As we begin our study of the tabernacle and the priest-hood, we must pause to consider a few preliminary matters.

First, because the Book of Exodus isn't arranged topically, information about the tabernacle and the priesthood is distributed throughout Exodus 25–39 as well as Leviticus, Numbers, and Deuteronomy. Perhaps God guided Moses to write it that way so the priests (and believers today) would have to read all the material in order to learn what God had to say. All Scripture is inspired of God and all Scripture must be considered as you study any topic. To make it easier to study these chapters, I've collated the material in Exodus under several major headings, and I'll also refer to the other three books of Moses.

Second, it would be easy to get detoured by examining every detail of every part of the tabernacle and the priestly garments, so I've focused on the major spiritual truths I believe God wants us to learn. Once you grasp these truths, you can study the other matters with more spiritual perception.

Finally, the tabernacle was a portable tent; it was not a place of assembly like a church building. Each time Israel broke camp, the Levites dismantled the tent carefully, wrapped the furnishings in their coverings, and carried them until the Lord told the people to stop. (The curtains and framework were carried on wagons.) At the new location, the tabernacle was reassembled and the furniture put into place (Num. 3–4). Each piece of furniture had rings attached through which poles were fitted so they could be carried in the wilderness march. The poles on the ark were never to be removed (Ex. 25:15; 1 Kings 8:8).

# T E N

EXODUS 24:9–25:40; 27:20-21;
30:11-16; 31:1-11;
35:4–36:38; 37:1-24; 38:21-31

## *The Place Where God Dwells— Part I*

Faithful to His promises in Exodus 6:6-8, the Lord delivered His people from Egypt (Ex. 1–18) and at Sinai "adopted" them to Himself as His special treasure (Ex. 19–24; Rom. 9:4). Now He was about to fulfill the rest of that promise by coming to the camp of Israel to dwell with His people (Ex. 25–40).

In order to do this, the Lord needed two things: a place for His glory to dwell and servants to minister to Him in that place. Therefore, He commanded the Jews to build the tabernacle and to set apart the tribe of Levi to serve Him. The building of the tabernacle and the ordaining of the priesthood are the two major themes of Exodus 25–40.

Throughout the Book of Genesis, the Lord had walked with His people—Adam and Eve (3:8), Enoch (5:22-24), Noah (6:9), and the patriarchs (17:1; 24:40; 48:15), but now He would *dwell* with them (Ex. 25:8, 45-46; 29:44-46). Having the Lord dwelling in the camp was a great privilege for the nation of Israel (Rom. 9:4-5), for no other nation had the living God in their midst. But the privilege brought with it a great responsibility, for it meant that the camp of Israel had to be a holy place where a holy God could dwell.

These sixteen chapters record much more than the historical events surrounding the construction of the tabernacle and the inauguration of the priesthood. What Moses wrote reveals some profound spiritual truths about a holy God and

# THE PLACE WHERE GOD DWELLS — PART I

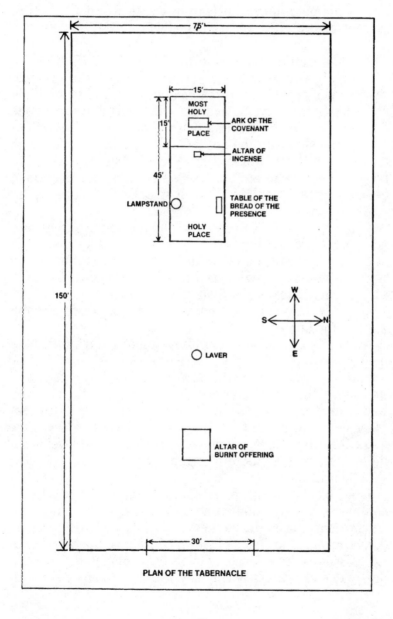

PLAN OF THE TABERNACLE

131

how we should approach Him in worship and serve Him "acceptably with reverence and godly fear" (Heb. 12:28).

## 1. God summons us to worship Him (Ex. 24:9-18)

Worshiping God is the highest privilege and the greatest responsibility of the Christian life, because God is the highest Being in the universe and the One to whom we must one day give account. Everything that we are and do flows out of our relationship with the Lord. God created us in His image so we might love Him and have fellowship with Him, not because we have to but because we want to. God is seeking people who will worship Him "in spirit and in truth" (John 4:23-24).

*Climbing higher.* At the base of the mountain, taking care not to get too close, the people of Israel waited for the words of the Lord. Moses, Aaron, Nadab and Abihu, and the seventy elders ascended higher and met with the Lord (Ex. 24:9-11), and then Moses and Joshua moved even higher (vv. 13-14). Finally, Moses alone went up higher and there saw the glory of the Lord (vv. 15-17).

All of this is an illustration of the important truth that we must grow in our worship experience with the Lord, *and we are the ones who decide how "high" we will go.* The people at the base of the mountain were afraid to hear God's voice and were satisfied to hear Moses speak to them (20:18-19), but Moses not only heard God's voice but saw God's glory! How tragic it is when God's people settle for the lowest level when there are new heights of blessing for those who seek God with their whole hearts.

Israel had to worship at a distance, because that was God's command, but God summons believers today to enter into His presence through "the new and living way" (Heb. 10:19-25). "Draw near to God and He will draw near to you" (James 4:8). We don't come fearfully to a stormy mountain but confidently to a glorious heavenly city where our names are written down as citizens of heaven (Heb. 12:18-24).

*Communing with God (Ex. 24:9-11).* When the Scripture says that the seventy-four men "saw God," this doesn't mean they beheld God in His essential being, for this isn't possible (John 1:18). They saw some of God's glory and they probably saw the throne of God on the sapphire pavement (see Ezek. 1:26), but the invisible God was hidden from them. After this vision of God, they shared a fellowship meal that climaxed the ratifying of the covenant. To eat together was a mark of friendship and agreement. God is glorious and high and lifted up, but He also condescends to fellowship with us![1]

*Tarrying with God (Ex. 24:12-18).* God called Moses to go even higher so that He might give him the tables of stone on which He had written the Ten Commandments. This is the first mention of the tables of the Law in Scripture. The glory cloud "abode" on Mt. Sinai, and the Hebrew word translated "abode" is *shekinah*, a word that both Jewish and Christian theologians use to describe the presence of God. It's translated "dwell" in 25:8 and 29:45-46. The blazing fire on the mount reminds us that "our God is a consuming fire" (Heb. 12:29). Moses remained on the mount with God for forty days and forty nights (see Matt. 4:1-2), and during that time, God gave him the plans for the tabernacle and the priesthood.

## 2. God designs the plan (Ex. 25:9, 40; 26:30)[2]

Whenever God does a work, He has a plan for that work, whether it's building the tabernacle or the temple (1 Chron. 28:11-12, 18-19), a local church (Phil. 2:12-13), or the individual Christian life and ministry (Eph. 2:10). God warned Moses to make everything according to the pattern revealed to him on the mount (Ex. 25:40; Heb. 8:5).

The earthly tabernacle was a copy of the heavenly tabernacle where our Lord now ministers to and for His people (Heb. 8:1-5; 9:1). The Book of Revelation mentions a brazen altar (6:9-11), an altar of incense (8:3-5), a throne (4:2), elders/priests (vv. 4-5), lamps (v. 5), a "sea" (v. 6), and cherubim (vv. 6-7), all of which parallel the main furnishings of the earthly tabernacle. It's a basic principle of ministry that we follow the pattern given from heaven, not the pattern of this world (Rom. 12:2).

### 3. God provides the materials (Ex. 25:1-9; 30:11-16; 35:4-29)

We can give to God only that which He has first given to us, for all things come from Him. "Everything comes from You," said David in his prayer, "and we have given You only what comes from Your hand" (1 Chron. 29:14, NIV).

Not only did God create the materials that the people brought to Him (Isa. 66:1-2), but He also worked in their hearts so that they were willing to give generously (see 2 Cor. 8:1-5, 12). In fact, the people brought so much that Moses had to tell them to stop! (Ex. 36:6-7)

Several different kinds of materials were needed: precious metals (gold, silver), bronze, fabrics (yarn, fine linen, and goat's hair), wood, skins, olive oil, spices, and precious stones. It's been estimated that a ton of gold was used in the tabernacle as well as over three tons of silver. Where did all this wealth come from? For one thing, the Jews had "spoiled" the Egyptians before leaving the land (12:35-36), and no doubt there were also spoils from the victory over Amalek (17:8-16). God saw to it that they had everything they needed to build the tabernacle just as He had designed it.

According to 30:11-16, Moses collected a half a shekel from each man of military age, and according to 38:21-31, all this silver amounted to 100 talents plus 1,775 shekels, a total of 301,775 shekels. (There are 3,000 shekels in a talent.) This came from 603,550 men who were twenty years of age and older. This silver was used to make both the sockets on which the posts stood and the hooks for the curtains.

**4. God equips the workers (Ex. 31:1-11; 35:30–36:7)**
Whether it's for building the tabernacle in the Old Testament, building the church in the New Testament, or building our lives and ministries today, the Holy Spirit of God must equip us and enable us to do the job. God gave Bezalel and Oholiab the skill and wisdom they needed, but He also equipped the craftsmen who worked under them, and led by the Spirit, in obedience to the Word, they constructed the tabernacle and its furniture.

God appointed Bezalel and Oholiab to direct the work, for without leaders there would be chaos, but He called for craftsmen to volunteer to assist them (35:10). We are born with different abilities, and at conversion, we received different gifts from the Holy Spirit, to be used for the good of the church and the glory of God (1 Cor. 12:1-13; Eph. 4:1-16; Rom. 12). "For it is God who works in you both to will and to do for His good pleasure" (Phil. 2:13, NKJV). The Jews built a tent that long ago turned to dust, but we're helping to build "a habitation of God in the Spirit" (Eph. 2:22) that will glorify God eternally.

**5. God must be put first in everything (Ex. 25:10-22; 37:1-9)**
There were six special pieces of furniture associated with the tabernacle and the ark of the covenant is mentioned first.[3] A wooden chest forty-five inches long, twenty-seven inches wide, and twenty-seven inches high, it stood in the holy of holies where God's "shekinah" presence rested. On it rested the golden mercy seat which was God's throne (Pss. 80:1; 99:1; 2 Kings 19:15, all NIV).

The ark had many names besides "the ark of the covenant" (Num. 10:33). It was called "the ark of God" (1 Sam. 3:3), "the ark of the Lord" (Josh. 3:15), "the ark of the Lord God" (1 Kings 2:26), "the ark of the testimony" (Ex. 25:22), because the tables of the Law were in it, "the holy ark" (2 Chron. 35:3), and "the ark of [God's] strength" (Ps. 132:8). The ark represented the power and authority of God in the camp of Israel, and this is why it's named first. This is the Old Testament illustration of Matthew 6:33.

The ark also teaches us about Jesus Christ. It was made of wood, which speaks of His humanity, but was completely overlaid with gold, which speaks of His deity. According to Hebrews 9:4, within the ark were the tables of the Law (Ex. 25:16), a pot of manna (16:32-34), and Aaron's rod that budded (Num. 16–17). These objects tell us that the Law of God was in Christ's heart and He perfectly obeyed and fulfilled it (Ps. 40:6-8; Heb. 10:5-9); He is the Bread of Life who gives eternal life to all who receive Him (John 6:32); and He lives by the power of an endless life so we can be fruitful for God (Heb. 7:16).

The golden mercy seat upon the ark had a cherub at each end and their wings overshadowed the ark. Once a year, on the Day of Atonement, the high priest was permitted to enter the holy of holies, where he sprinkled the blood of the sacrifices on the mercy seat (Lev. 16). This made atonement for Israel's sins for another year (vv. 29-34). The fulfillment of this type was when Jesus Christ died once for all for the sins of the world and took away sin by the sacrifice of Himself (Heb. 9:11–10:14).

Frequently in Scripture you find the image of finding safety "under His wings." Sometimes this refers to the mother bird protecting her young (Pss. 57:1; 63:7; Matt. 23:37; Luke 13:34), but it can also refer to being under the wings of the cherubim in the holy of holies (Ruth 2:12; Pss. 17:8; 36:7-8; 61:4; 91:1, 4).

Moses was permitted to enter the holy of holies where God spoke to him from the mercy seat and revealed His will for the people of Israel (Ex. 25:21-22; 29:42; 30:6, 36; Num. 7:89; see Ps. 91:1). God's people today have access into God's presence through the blood of Jesus Christ (Heb. 10:19-25), for He is our "mercy seat" (propitiation, Rom. 3:25; 1 John 2:2). Because of His blood shed for us, the throne of God is for us a throne of grace.

The ark of the Lord and the pillar of cloud led the way as the Jews marched from place to place (Num. 10:33-36). In their pilgrim journey, the people of God get their directions from the throne of God and follow the glory of God.

## 6. God is present to nourish His people (Ex. 25:23-29; 37:10-16)

As the priest walked into the holy place from the outer court, on the right he would see the table of "presence bread," on the left the golden lampstand, and ahead of him the golden altar of incense standing before the beautiful veil that separated the holy place from the holy of holies.

The table was three feet long, a foot and a half wide and twenty-seven inches high. Like the ark, it was made of acacia wood covered with gold, another reminder of our Savior's humanity and deity. Jesus is the Bread of Life who took upon Himself a human body that He might come to this earth and die for our sins (John 6:26).

Twelve loaves of bread were baked each week, following the recipe given in Leviticus 24:5-9. The text doesn't explain how big these loaves were, but from the amount of flour required, they must have been quite large.[4] It's likely that the flour was provided by the people as a gift to the Lord. Each Sabbath, the old loaves were removed and eaten by the priests in the holy place, and the new loaves were put in their place.

When the bread was placed on the table, it was always accompanied by incense, which was probably burned in one of the special utensils (Ex. 25:29). The use of incense suggests that the bread was actually a "meal offering" to the Lord (Lev. 2:1-11) in thanksgiving to Him for "daily bread." If the flour was a gift from the people, it was their sacrifice of thanksgiving to God for His provision for their needs.

The loaves are called "showbread" (Ex. 25:30) or "presence bread," literally "bread of faces." The presence of twelve loaves of bread in the holy place couldn't help but remind the priests that they were serving the twelve tribes of Israel, God's chosen people. Through these loaves, the twelve tribes were presented before God and God was present with them in their camp, beholding their worship and their daily walk. The tribes were also represented by the jewels on the breastplate and the shoulders of the high priest (28:6-21). When you combine the images of the jewels and the loaves, you learn that the Lord feeds His people, bears them on His shoulders, and carries them over His heart.

But there's also a sense in which the loaves remind us that Israel was called to feed a hungry world the spiritual bread the Lord had given them. They gave the world the Word of God, which is bread (Matt. 4:4), and Jesus who is the Bread of Life (John 6). Unfortunately, they turned from the Lord and ate at heathen altars, and God had to discipline them.

Paul compared the church to a loaf of unleavened bread (1 Cor. 5:1-8; see 10:16-17), and our task is to preach the Word and tell sinners about Jesus Christ, the Bread of Life. Since the twelve loaves were considered a meal offering, there would have been no leaven in the dough (Lev. 2:1-11), and God's people must keep themselves from all impurity. We aren't here to feed ourselves; we're here to feed a hungry world.

The loaves of bread were very special and were not to be eaten carelessly, even by the priests. Any priest who was defiled and ate the bread or any of the sacrificial meat that belonged to the priests, was in danger of death (Lev. 22:3-9).

## 7. God enlightens our worship and service (Ex. 25:31-40; 27:20-21; 37:17-24; Lev. 24:1-3)

The candlestick was hammered out of about seventy-five

pounds of gold, but we aren't told its dimensions. It was undoubtedly a beautiful work of art with its six branches decorated with almond flowers, buds, and blossoms. The six branches and the central shaft provided seven lamps which were fed by oil and kept burning constantly (Ex. 27:20-21; Lev. 24:1-4).[5]

Since there was no way to let in natural light from the outside, the golden lampstand was the only source of light available in the holy place. Without it, the priests couldn't have carried on their various ministries. God wants us to offer Him intelligent worship, not ignorant worship (John 4:19-24; Acts 17:22-31; Rom. 1:18-25), and to do that, we need the light of the Word of God to guide us (Ps. 119:105, 130; Prov. 6:23).

Aaron and his sons were to trim the lamps each time they offered the incense on the golden altar (Ex. 30:7-8). We shall see later that the fragrant burning incense represents prayer ascending to God, and the Word of God and prayer must go together (Acts 6:4): Prayer is enlightened by the Word (John 15:7), and the Word is opened up to us as we pray (Ps. 119:18; Eph. 1:15-23). Both the study of the Word and the exercise of prayer must be energized by the Holy Spirit, who is symbolized by oil (the lampstand, Zech. 4:1-7) and fire (the altar, Acts 2:3-4).

But the candlestick also reminds us of the people of Israel, chosen by God to be "a light to the Gentiles" (Isa. 42:6; 49:6). However, the lampstand wasn't in the outer court of the tabernacle where everybody could see it, but in the holy place where only God and the priests could see it. How, then, does it symbolize Israel's witness to the Gentiles? *Israel's relationship to God in sacrifice and worship determined the strength and extent of their witness.* It was when they turned from the worship of the true and living God and began to worship idols that they lost their witness to the Gentile nations.

Jesus Christ also came to be a "light to the Gentiles" (Luke 1:79; John 8:12), and that light is spread through the witness of the church (Acts 13:47-48; Phil. 2:14-16; Matt. 5:14-16). In Revelation 1:9-20, our Lord stands in the midst of seven lampstands which represent the seven churches of Asia Minor in John's day. In the tabernacle, there was one lampstand, beaten out of one talent of gold, representing the one nation of Israel and its witness. Though the church is one people, it spreads the light through many individual assemblies in many places in the world.

The lights in the seven lamps on the lampstand were fed by oil that was especially prepared for that purpose (Ex. 27:20-21). Just as the people brought the fine flour for the baking of the loaves, so they brought clear oil for the maintaining of the lights on the lampstand (Ex. 25:27-28; 35:10, 14). Zechariah 4:1-4 informs us that this oil symbolizes the Holy Spirit of God, without whose power we can't glorify Christ (John 16:14) or effectively witness of Him (Acts 1:8). "Without Me," said Jesus, "you can do nothing" (John 15:5, NKJV).

What was done by the priests in the sanctuary was done for the Lord (Ex. 28:1, 3-4, 41; 29:1) and before the Lord (27:21; 40:25; Lev. 24:4). It mattered not that the people in the camp were ignorant of what the priests were doing, because God saw it all, and their task was to please Him. *The most important part of a Christian's life is the part that only God sees.* If God is pleased by what He sees, and our conscience is clean before Him, then we don't have to worry about what people think or say about us (1 Cor. 4:1-5). He will accept our ministry and bless it.

EXODUS 26:1-37; 27:1-19; 30:1-10,
17-21; 37:25-29; 38:1-20

# The Place Where God Dwells—
# Part II

We have three more pieces of tabernacle furniture to study: the incense altar; the laver; and the brazen altar. Then we want to look at the tabernacle structure itself, the framework, the coverings, and the veils. As we study, our emphasis will continue to be on the God of the tabernacle and what He does for His people.

## 1. God hears the prayers of His people (Ex. 30:1-10, 34-38; 37:25-29)

The altar of incense was made of acacia wood overlaid with gold, and was a foot and a half square and three feet high. It was the tallest piece of furniture in the holy place. It had an ornamental gold rim ("crown") around the top and golden "horns" at each corner. It stood before the veil that separated the holy of holies from the holy place, and the priest burned incense on it each morning and evening when he trimmed the lamps.

In the Bible, burning incense is often a picture of prayer. "Let my prayer be set forth before Thee as incense," David prayed (Ps. 141:2), and John saw the elders in heaven with "golden bowls full of incense, which are the prayers of the saints" (Rev. 5:8; see 8:3-4).[1] Whenever the priest burned the incense, it was a call to the people for a time of prayer (Luke 1:8-10).

The fire for burning the incense came from the brazen altar where the sacrifices were offered to God (Lev. 16:12-13; Num. 16:46). This suggests that true prayer must be based on the work of Christ on the cross and on our complete dedication to God. A true fervency in prayer isn't a religious emotion we work up ourselves; rather, it's a blessing that God sends down as we yield ourselves to Him. John Bunyan, author of *The Pilgrim's Progress*, said, "In prayer it is better to have a heart without words, than words without a heart." Coldhearted praying is not effective praying (James 5:16).

In order to please God and not be in danger of death, the priest had to use not only the right fire on the altar but also the prescribed mixture of spices for the incense (Ex. 30:34-38). Nadab and Abihu tried to worship God with "false fire" and were killed (Lev. 10). Any Israelite who tried to duplicate this special incense for his own personal use would be cut off, which could mean death.

Prayer isn't simply a jumble of words we mix together with the hope they'll be heard by God and answered. The Bible names some of the "ingredients" of prayer—adoration, confession, thanksgiving, petition, submission (1 Tim. 2:1; Phil. 4:6)—and even gives us a pattern to follow (Matt. 6:5-15).[2] You can be sure that the priest didn't rush into the tabernacle, quickly burn the incense, and then rush out. No, he prepared himself and reverently approached the altar, knowing that he was in the presence of a holy God.

Because of the work of Christ on the cross, believers today can go through the veil into the very presence of God, and there present their worship and petitions in the name of Jesus (Heb. 10:19-25). Our living, reigning Priest-King, Jesus Christ, is interceding continually for us in heaven (Rom. 8:33-34; Heb. 4:14-16; 7:19-28), and the Holy Spirit also intercedes in our hearts (Rom. 8:26-27). While it's good to open and close the day with special prayer, as the priests did, it's also good to "pray without ceasing" (1 Thes. 5:17) and stay in communion with the Lord all during the day.

The priests were warned not to use this golden altar for anything other than burning incense (Ex. 30:9), for there are no substitutes for prayer. No amount of sacrificing can take the place of true praying. The golden altar wasn't a place for making bargains with God or trying to change His mind (James 4:1-4; 1 John 5:14-15). It was a place for adoring Him and praying, "Thy will be done."

It's worth noting that the special incense had to be "salted" (Ex. 30:35, NIV), for salt is a symbol of purity and of a covenant relationship (Lev. 2:13). "If I regard iniquity in my heart, the Lord will not hear" (Ps. 66:18, NKJV). We're commanded to lift up "holy hands" as we pray, and to remove "anger or disputing" from our hearts (1 Tim. 2:8, NIV). If God killed every believer today who didn't pray as He has ordered, how many of us would survive a prayer meeting?[3]

Once a year, on the Day of Atonement, the priest had to apply blood to the incense altar in order to make it ceremonially clean before God (Ex. 30:10). Even in our praying we can sin!

## 2. God receives His people's sacrifices (Ex. 27:1-8; 38:1-7)

When a worshiper came to the tabernacle to offer a sacrifice, the first thing he met was a white linen fence, 150 feet long and 75 feet wide, that surrounded the tabernacle and created a courtyard area where the priests ministered. The tabernacle proper stood at the west end of this courtyard, and at the east end was a 30-foot entrance to the enclosure. Here the priests met the people who came to offer sacrifices and examined each animal carefully to make sure it was acceptable. The worshiper would put his hand on the animal's head to identify with the offering (Lev. 1:1-9), and then the priest would slay the animal and offer it on the brazen altar according to the regulations given in Leviticus 1–7.[4]

There was only one entrance to the enclosure and therefore only one way to get to the altar of God. When God puts up a fence and assigns the way in, nobody has the authority to question it or change it. Jesus claimed to be the only door (John 10:9) and the only way to God (14:6), which explains why Peter said, "Nor is there salvation in any other, for there is no other name under heaven given among men by which we must be saved" (Acts 4:12, NKJV). In today's pluralistic society, many people like to think that every way is acceptable to God, but that attitude leads to death (Prov. 14:12; 16:25; Matt. 7:13-27).

The brazen altar was a hollow "box," seven and a half feet wide and four and a half feet high, made of acacia wood covered with bronze. In Scripture, bronze is often identified with judgment (Num. 21:4-9; Deut. 28:23; Rev. 1:15). Two and a half feet from the top, inside the "box," was a bronze grating on which the priests kept a fire burning (Lev. 6:8-13) and through which the ashes of the wood and the sacrifices fell. Because they were part of offerings dedicated to God, these ashes were considered ceremonially clean and were collected on the east side of the altar. Regularly, the priests carried these ashes outside the camp to a clean place (1:16; 4:12; 6:10-11).

Unlike the golden altar of incense in the holy place, the brazen altar was a place of bloodshed and death, for "without the shedding of blood there is no forgiveness" (Heb. 9:22, NIV). If a sinner could manage to enter the tabernacle courtyard and wash in the laver, that wouldn't save him, nor would he be forgiven if he entered the holy place and ate the bread or burned the incense. *The way into the presence of God began at the brazen altar where innocent victims died for guilty sinners.* In short, the brazen altar takes us immediately to

Calvary where the Son of God died for the sins of the world (Matt. 26:26-28; John 1:29; 3:14-16; Rom. 5:8; 1 Peter 2:24).

Each morning, the priests were to offer a burnt offering on the brazen altar (Ex. 29:42-43), a picture of total dedication to the Lord (Lev. 1). That would be a good way for each of God's children to begin the day, presenting ourselves in total dedication to God as "living sacrifices" (Rom. 12:1-2).

Preachers and evangelists sometimes invite people in their congregations to "come to the altar," but there are no altars on earth that are ordained of God or acceptable to God. Why? Because the death of Jesus Christ took care of the sin problem once and for all (Heb. 9:25-28). No more sacrifices can be or should be offered. The Lord's Supper (Communion, Eucharist) is a reminder of His sacrifice, not a repeat of His sacrifice.

The only "altar" believers have today is Jesus Christ Himself who bears on His glorified body the wounds of the cross (Heb. 13:10; Luke 24:39; John 20:20). As a holy priesthood, believers "offer up spiritual sacrifices acceptable to God *through Jesus Christ*" (1 Peter 2:5, NKJV, italics mine). We present to Him our bodies (Rom. 12:1-2), our material wealth (Phil. 4:18), praise and good works (Heb. 13:15-16), and a broken heart (Ps. 51:17).

### 3. God wants His people to be clean (Ex. 30:17-21; 38:8)

In the tabernacle courtyard, the laver stood between the brazen altar and the tent, and the priests and Levites had to stop there regularly to wash their hands and feet. If they entered the tent or served at the brazen altar without first washing, they were in danger of death.

The Lord didn't specify either the size or shape of the laver, nor do the instructions say anything about how it was carried when the nation was moving to a new location. The size and shape of the laver wasn't the important thing; it was the contents of the laver that really mattered. It held clean water, and the supply was replenished all day long by the Levites.

In Scripture, water for *drinking* is a picture of the Spirit of God (John 7:37-39), while water for *washing* is a picture of the Word of God (Ps. 119:9; John 15:3; Eph. 5:25-27). The laver, then, typifies the Word of God that cleanses the mind and heart of those who receive it and obey it (John 17:17). The fact that the laver was made out of the bronze mirrors of the Jewish women (Ex. 38:8) is evidence that it typifies God's Word, for the Word of God is compared to a mirror (James 1:22-26; 2 Cor. 3:18).

Under the Old Testament economy, there were three ways to achieve ceremonial cleansing: by water, by fire, or by blood. We are cleansed from the guilt of sin by the blood of Jesus Christ shed for us on the cross, and when we confess our sins, that blood cleanses us (1 John 1:5–2:2). But when we disobey God, our hearts and minds are *defiled* by sin (see Ps. 51), and it's the "washing of the word" (Eph. 5:26) that restores us.

But the Old Testament priests became defiled, not by sinning against God but by *serving* God! Their feet became dirty as they walked in the courtyard and in the tabernacle (there was no floor in the tabernacle), and their hands were defiled as they handled the sacrifices and sprinkled the blood. Therefore, their hands and feet needed constant cleansing, and this was provided at the laver.

When He was with them in the Upper Room, our Lord taught His disciples this same lesson by washing their feet (John 13:1-15).[5] When we trust Christ to save us, we're "washed all over" (v. 10; 1 Cor. 6:9-11) and don't require another bath, but as we go through life, our feet get dirty and we need to be cleansed. If we aren't cleansed, we can't have fellowship with the Lord (John 13:8), and if we're out of fellowship with the Lord, we can't enjoy His love or do His will. When we confess our sins, He cleanses us, and when we meditate on the Word, the Spirit renews us and restores us.

Twice David prayed, "Wash me" (Ps. 51:2, 7), and God answered that prayer (2 Sam. 12:13). But Isaiah told the sinners of his day, "Wash and make yourselves clean" (Isa. 1:16, NIV), which suggests that we need to clean up our own lives and put away the things that defile us. Paul had this in mind when he wrote, "Let us cleanse ourselves from all filthiness of the flesh and spirit, perfecting holiness in the fear of God" (2 Cor. 7:1).

For the priests, washing in the laver wasn't a luxury; it was a necessity. Keeping themselves clean was a matter of life and death!

**4. God wants His people to appreciate and enjoy His blessings (Ex. 26:1-37; 27:9-19; 36:8-38; 38:9-20)**
"Honor and majesty are before Him," wrote the psalmist; "strength and beauty are in His sanctuary" (Ps. 96:6). The strength of His sanctuary is revealed in its *construction*, and the beauty is revealed in its *adornment*.

*Strength.* The tabernacle proper was a solid structure over which the beautiful curtains were draped. Twenty boards of acacia wood, fifteen feet high and twenty-seven inches wide, overlaid with gold, formed the north and south walls, and eight similar boards formed the west wall. Each of these boards stood on two silver bases made from the shekels ("redemption money") collected from the Jewish men of military age. Since the structure stood on the uneven ground, these bases were necessary for stability and security. God's sanctuary didn't rest on the shifting sands of this world but on the solid foundation of redemption. The forty-eight boards were further strengthened by four long rods (cross-bars) that ran through golden rings on each board.

At the east end of the tabernacle stood five posts on which a linen curtain hung, beautifully embroidered with blue, purple, and scarlet yarn. This was the door into the holy place. Some students believe that a rod ran straight through the boards of the north and south walls, connecting them to the end pillars and adding even more stability to the framework.

*Beauty.* Gold, blue, purple, scarlet, and white are the major colors used in the hangings and coverings of the tabernacle.[6] The linen fence around the sacred area was white, reminding us of the holiness of God. The thirty-foot gate at the east end of the tabernacle was embroidered with blue, purple, and scarlet against the white background. Blue is the color of the sky and reminds us of heaven and the God of heaven. Purple is the royal color that speaks of the King, and scarlet makes us think of blood and the sacrifice of the Savior.

The holy place and holy of holies were covered with four different coverings (curtains) that draped over the walls and hung down to the ground. People looking at the tabernacle would see the leatherlike outmost covering composed of badgers' skins ("sea cows," NIV), which protected the other coverings as well as the tabernacle proper and its furnishings. Beneath that protective covering was a curtain of rams' skins dyed red, then a fabric woven of goats' hair, which may well have been black, and last of all a beautiful covering of fine linen embroidered with cherubim in blue, purple, and scarlet.

Between the holy place and the holy of holies, the veil hung from golden clasps, supported by four pillars. It was embroidered with cherubim in white, scarlet, blue, and purple. Hebrews 10:20 says that this veil typifies the body of Christ, for when His body was offered on the cross, the veil of the temple was torn from top to bottom (Mark 15:38). Some students see a parallel between the four Gospels and the four pillars that supported the veil with the four colors. Purple speaks of royalty—the Gospel of Matthew, the Gospel of the King. Scarlet reminds us of sacrifice—the Gospel of Mark, the Gospel of the Suffering Servant. White speaks of the perfect Son of Man—the Gospel of Luke, and blue points to heaven—the Gospel of John, the Gospel of the Son of God who came from heaven to die for our sins.

*Appreciation.* No matter how common the tabernacle may have appeared to outsiders, everything within the sanctuary was costly and beautiful, and it all spoke of the Savior who the people of Israel would give to the world.

Godly believers in the Old Testament realized the treasures they possessed in God's house. Listen to David's testimony:

> One thing have I desired of the Lord, that will I
> seek after: that I may dwell in the house of the
> Lord all the days of my life, to behold the beauty
> of the Lord, and to inquire in His temple (Ps. 27:4).
> Lord, I have loved the habitation of Your house, and
> the place where Your glory dwells (26:8, NKJV).
> We shall be satisfied with the goodness of Your
> house, of Your holy temple (65:4, NKJV).

And the sons of Korah wrote:

> How lovely is Your tabernacle, O Lord of hosts!
> My soul longs, yes, even faints for the courts of the
> Lord; my heart and my flesh cry out for the living
> God. . . . Blessed are those who dwell in Your house;
> they will be still praising You (84:1-2, 4, NKJV).

What Old Testament believers had in the tabernacle, and later in the temple, God's people today have in Jesus Christ.

The furnishings and the ceremonies point to Christ and reveal the many glorious aspects of His character and the salvation He gives to all who trust Him. Every spiritual need of the Jewish people was met in the provisions of the tabernacle, and in Jesus Christ we have everything that we need "for life and godliness" (2 Peter 1:3).

Any approach to the Christian life that adds anything to the person and work of Jesus Christ as revealed in Scripture is not the right approach. All fullness dwells in Christ (Col. 1:19) as well as all the fullness of the Godhead (2:9). In Christ are "hidden all the treasures of wisdom and knowledge" (v. 3), and we must "seek those things which are above, where Christ is, sitting at the right hand of God" (3:1, NKJV). In Christ God's people have every spiritual blessing (Eph. 1:3), and He is all they need.

To the believers who loved God and wanted to please Him, the holy sanctuary was the source of food and drink for their souls. "Both high and low among men find refuge in the shadow of Your wings [the holy of holies]. They feast on the abundance of Your house" (Ps. 36:7-8).

In like manner, believers today feast on Jesus Christ and find in Him all the satisfaction they need.

# T W E L V E

# *The Holy Priesthood*

It was God's desire that the nation of Israel be "a kingdom of priests" (19:6) in the world, revealing His glory and sharing His blessings with the unbelieving nations around them. But in order to magnify a holy God, Israel had to be a holy people, and that's where the Aaronic priesthood came in. It was the task of the priests (Aaron's family) and the Levites (the families of Kohath, Gershon, and Merari; see Num. 3–4) to serve in the tabernacle and represent the people before God. The priests were also to represent God to the people by teaching them the Law and helping them to obey it (Lev. 10:8-11; Deut. 33:10; Mal. 2:7).

But Israel failed to live like a kingdom of priests. Instead, the spiritual leadership in the nation gradually deteriorated until the priests actually permitted the people to worship idols in the temple of God! (Ezek. 8) The Lord punished His people by allowing the Babylonians to destroy Jerusalem and the temple and carry thousands of Jews into exile. Why did this happen? "But it happened because of the sins of her prophets and the iniquities of her priests, who shed within her the blood of the righteous" (Lam. 4:13, NIV).

Today, God wants His church to minister in this world as a "holy priesthood" and a "royal priesthood" (1 Peter 2:5, 9).[1] If God's people are faithful in their priestly ministry, they will "proclaim the praises of Him who called [them] out of dark-

151

ness into His marvelous light" (1 Peter 2:9, NKJV). As we study the Old Testament priesthood, you will see significant parallels between the work of the Jewish priests in the past and the ministry of "the holy priesthood" in the church today.[2]

## 1. Priests are chosen to serve God (Ex. 28:1, 3, 41; 29:1, 44)

The Lord's words "to minister unto Me" are found five times in these two chapters, and also in 30:30; 40:13, 15; Leviticus 7:35. To be sure, the priests ministered to the people, but their first obligation was to minister to the Lord and please Him. If they forgot their obligation to the Lord, they would soon begin to minimize their responsibilities to the people, and the nation would decay spiritually. (See Mal. 1:6–2:9.)

That God chose Aaron and his sons to minister in the priesthood was an act of sovereign grace, because they certainly didn't earn this position or deserve it. But, that God should save sinners like us, make us His children, and form us into a "holy priesthood" is also an act of His grace, and we should never lose the wonder of this spiritual privilege. "You did not choose Me, but I chose you" (John 15:16, NKJV).

It's unfortunate that Nadab and Abihu disobeyed the Lord and were killed (Lev. 10). When Aaron died, Eleazer became his successor (Num. 20:22-29); and Ithamar's descendants continued in priestly ministry even after the Captivity (Ezra 8:1-2).

God's people today must remember that our first obligation is to please the Lord and serve Him. If we do this, then He will work in us and through us to accomplish His work in this world. When Jesus restored Peter to discipleship, He didn't ask "Do you love the ministry?" or even "Do you love people?" His repeated question was, "Do you love Me?" (John 21:17) Just as a father's most important obligation is to love his children's mother, so the servant's most important obligation (and privilege) is to love the Lord. All ministry flows out of that relationship.

A part of pleasing the Lord was wearing the priestly garments. The high priest, the priests, and the Levites couldn't dress as they pleased when they ministered at the tabernacle; they had to wear the garments God designed for them. God provided these garments for at least three reasons: (1) they gave the priests "dignity and honor" (Ex. 28:2, NIV) and set them apart, just as a uniform identifies a soldier or a nurse; (2) they revealed spiritual truths relating to their ministry and our ministry today; and (3) if the priests didn't wear the special garments, they might die (vv. 35, 43).

## 2. Priests are chosen to serve the people (Ex. 28:6-30)

In serving God and the people, the high priest wore seven pieces of clothing: undergarments (vv. 42-43); a white inner robe ("coat"; v. 39; 39:27; Lev. 8:6-7); a blue robe over that, with bells and pomegranates on the hem (Ex. 28:31-35; 39:22-26); the ephod, a sleeveless garment of gold, blue, purple, and scarlet, held together by a jeweled clasp on each shoulder (28:6-8; 39:1-5; Lev. 8:7); a girdle at the waist (Ex. 28:8); a jeweled breastplate, held in place on the ephod by golden chains attached to the shoulder clasps (vv. 9-30; 39:8-21); and a white linen turban ("miter," 28:39) with a golden plate on it that said "Holy to the Lord" (v. 36, NIV).

*The ephod and girdle (Ex. 28:6-14; 39:2-7).* "Ephod" is the transliteration of a Hebrew word for a simple sleeveless linen garment that reached to the ankles, usually associated with religious service (1 Sam. 2:18; 2 Sam. 6:14). The high priest's ephod and girdle were made of white linen beautifully embroidered with blue, purple, and scarlet threads. The ephod was of two pieces, front and back, held together on each shoulder by a jeweled golden clasp and at the waist by the beautiful girdle.

The significant thing about this ephod was not the fabric or the colors. It was that the names of six tribes of Israel were engraved on each onyx stone on the shoulder clasps, according to their birth order. Whenever the high priest wore his special robes, he carried the people on his shoulders before the Lord. Furthermore, these two onyx stones reminded him of two important facts: (1) the tribes of Israel were precious in the sight of God; (2) he wasn't in the tabernacle to display his beautiful robes or to exalt his special position, but to represent the people before the Lord and carry them on his shoulders. He had been called, not to serve himself but to serve his people.[3]

If the church is to be faithful as a holy priesthood, believers must serve Christ by serving one another and serving a lost world. Jesus said, "I am among you as the One who serves" (Luke 22:27), and it's His example that we should follow (John 13:12-17). In the high-powered spiritual atmosphere of the tabernacle, it would be easy for the priest to ignore the common people outside, many of whom had burdens and problems and needed God's help. "Let each of you look out not only for his own interests, but also for the interests of others" (Phil. 2:4, NKJV).

*The breastplate (Ex. 28:15-30; 39:8-21).* The breastplate was a piece of beautifully embroidered fabric, nine inches square when folded double. It hung on the high priest's chest, supported by two golden chains attached to the shoulder clasps. On the breastplate were twelve beautiful jewels, arranged in four rows, each stone representing one of the tribes of Israel. The stones were probably arranged according to the order of the tribes as they marched (28:21; see Num. 10).

So the high priest not only carried the people on his shoulders, but he also carried them over his heart. If we don't have sincere love in our hearts, we won't be concerned about the needs of others, and we won't want to help them. "My little children, let us not love in word, neither in tongue; but in deed and in truth" (1 John 4:18). As servants of God, we should be able to say honestly to the people we serve, "I have you in my heart" (Phil. 1:7).

The variety of stones on the breastplate suggests the variety of people in the church and in the world, all of them precious to God. Each of the tribes had its own distinctive outlook and personality, and no two were alike. Some were quick to go to battle, while some stayed home (Jud. 5:13-18). Some were easy to work with while others liked to argue and be important (Jud. 8). Yet the Lord loved them all and the high priest had to minister to them all.

"Pastoring a church would be a wonderful experience if it weren't for people!" a young minister said to me. I reminded him that helping people and meeting their spiritual needs is what ministry is all about, and this demands a great deal of patient love on our part. We are a "holy priesthood" and a "royal priesthood," but we must constantly be a "loving priesthood."

Within the folded breastplate were kept "the Urim and Thummim" ("lights and perfections") which the high priest used to determine the will of God for the nation (Ex. 28:30; Num. 27:21; 1 Sam. 30:7-8). We don't know what the procedure was, but it was the priests' duty to perform it (Deut. 33:8; Ezra 2:63; Neh. 7:65). Some think there were two stones in the pouch, one black and one white, and the stone the priest withdrew indicated the will of God. Or perhaps they were jewels that shone in a special way to indicate the leading of the Lord. It's useless to speculate because the details haven't been revealed to us.

Believers today don't have devices such as the Urim and

Thummim for determining what God wants us to do, but we do have the Word of God to guide our steps (Ps. 119:105). The Word of God reveals the God of the Word, His character, His desires, and His purposes for His people, and the better we know God, the better we can discover His will. God's Word contains precepts for us to obey, warnings for us to heed, promises for us to claim, and principles for us to follow. If we're sincerely willing to obey, God is willing to direct us (John 7:17; Ps. 25:8-11).

But if we had a simple infallible method of determining the will of God such as the Urim and Thummim, we probably wouldn't pray as much, search the Scriptures as much, or humble ourselves as much as we do today as we seek God's direction. But seeking and doing God's will is the way we grow in the Lord, and sharing in the process is as much a blessing as knowing the results.

### 3. Priests must serve in the fear of God (Ex. 28:31-43; 39:22-31)

Moses enumerates some additional articles of clothing.

*The blue robe (Ex. 28:31-35; 39:22-26)*, worn under the ephod, was distinctive in at least three ways. For one thing, it was seamless, reminding us of our Lord's seamless robe that symbolized His perfect character and integrity (John 19:23). The collar around the opening for the head was woven so that it would not tear. During our Lord's ministry on earth, some people tried to "tear" the seamless robe of His character and accuse Him of wrong, but they never succeeded. Finally, around the hem of this garment hung pomegranates made of blue, purple, and scarlet yarn, with golden bells hanging between them. The pomegranates symbolized fruitfulness and the golden bells gave witness that the high priest was ministering in the holy place.[4] The bells and pomegranates remind us that our priestly walk must be fruitful and faithful, always giving witness that we're serving the Lord with integrity.

*The turban (Ex. 28:36-38; 39:27-31)* was worn only by the high priest, while the other priests wore linen bonnets. At the front of the turban was the golden plate that read "Holiness to the Lord" ("Holy to the Lord," NIV). The whole purpose of the levitical system was to make men and women holy and therefore pleasing to the Lord.

It comes as a shock to some people to learn that Jesus did not die to make us happy; He died to make sinners holy. "Be holy, for I am holy" was a frequent command to the Jews (Lev. 11:44-45; 19:2; 20:7, 26; 21:8) and it's repeated in 1 Peter 1:15-16 for believers today. *The first step toward happiness is holiness.* If we're right with God, then we can start being right with others and with the circumstances of life that trouble us. If you aim for happiness, you'll miss it, but if you aim for holiness, you'll also find happiness in the Lord.

In wearing this holy turban and its gold "crown," the high priest identified himself with the sins of the people as they brought their offerings to the Lord (Ex. 28:38). Just as Christians bring their holy sacrifices to God through Jesus Christ, and this makes the sacrifices acceptable (1 Peter 2:5), so the gifts of the people were acceptable to God because of the intercession of the high priest. However, our Lord and Intercessor in heaven doesn't need any special garments or "holy crowns" to qualify for ministry, because He is the holy Son of God, and in Him there is no sin.

Twice in this section the priests are warned that they might die if they didn't fully obey the Lord's instructions and wear the right garments (Ex. 28:35, 43). In other words, God's servants must walk in the fear of the Lord and be careful to obey Him and give Him the glory.

Nobody who is working wholeheartedly for the Lord will deny that "there is joy in serving Jesus," but at the same time, we must cultivate "reverence and godly fear" (Heb. 12:28). If the Lord killed every believer today who didn't enter seriously into his or her service, how many workers would be left? Fearing the Lord doesn't mean cringing before a hard taskmaster so much as being reverent and humble before a loving Father and gracious Lord. "Serve the Lord with fear, and rejoice with trembling" (Ps. 2:11, NKJV). "'A son honors his father, and a servant his master. If I am a father, where is the honor due Me? If I am a master, where is the respect due Me?' says the Lord Almighty" (Mal. 1:6).

We have already noted that the priests would die if they failed to wash at the laver (Ex. 30:20-21) or if they used a different incense from that which was ordered by God (Lev. 16:13). If the priests didn't obey the laws concerning the clean and unclean, they were also in danger of death (22:1-9). It wasn't enough for the priests to teach the people the Law; they had to be careful to obey it themselves, because they had the greater responsibility. But the basic attitude that helps to determine our obedience is a Spirit-inspired fear of the Lord.

I've attended some Christian "worship" services and evangelistic meetings where the main emphasis was "having a good time" and not glorifying God. The music was entertaining but not edifying, and the preaching was shallow and flippant. The speakers were more concerned with getting the crowd to laugh than with helping them to see Jesus and repent of their sins. God didn't kill anybody at these meetings, but we didn't sense the life and power of the Spirit in what went on. Because the participants weren't focused on honoring God, the meeting killed itself.

### 4. Priests must be consecrated to God (Ex. 29:1-37; 30:22-33)
God commanded that the high priest and his sons participate

in a public consecration service that would set them apart as God's servants. There were at least seven stages in this service.

*The priests were washed (Ex. 29:4; Lev. 8:6).* Moses gathered the materials that were needed for the ordination service and brought Aaron and his sons to the door of the tabernacle. The erecting of the tabernacle isn't described until Exodus 40, but it appears that the dedication of the tabernacle and the consecration of the priests occurred on the same day (vv. 12-15).

Sin is pictured by many images in the Bible, such as disease (Isa. 1:4-6), darkness (1 John 1:5-10), drowning (Ps. 130:1-4), and even death (Eph. 2:1, 5; John 5:24), but frequently it's pictured as dirt and defilement (Isa. 1:16, 18; Jer. 4:14; 2 Cor. 7:1; Heb. 9:14; James 1:21; 4:8). When Aaron and his sons were washed all over, it was symbolic of complete cleansing from the Lord. They didn't have to be bathed all over again; all they had to do was cleanse their hands and feet at the laver. "A person who has had a bath needs only to wash his feet; his whole body is clean," said Jesus (John 13:10, NIV). Those who have trusted Christ have experienced this inward cleansing from the Lord (1 Cor. 6:9-11).

*The priests were clothed (Ex. 29:5-6, 8-9, 29-30; Lev. 8:7-9, 13).* Moses clothed his brother with the garments we've been studying, and he also clothed Aaron's sons with their linen tunics and bonnets. These were their official "uniforms" and they dared not minister in the tabernacle dressed in other garments.

In Scripture, the wearing of garments is a picture of the character and life of the believer. We're to lay aside the filthy garments of the old life and wear the beautiful "garments of grace" provided by the Lord (Eph. 4:17-32; Col. 3:1-15). Christ has taken away our dirty rags and given us a robe of righteousness that He purchased for us on the cross (Isa.

61:10; 2 Cor. 5:17, 21).

*The priests were anointed (Ex. 29:7, 21; Lev. 8:10-12, 30).* This special oil (Ex. 30:22-33) was used only to anoint the priests and the tabernacle and its furnishings. In the Old Testament, prophets, priests, and kings were anointed; it was a symbol that God had granted them the Holy Spirit for power and service (Luke 4:17-19; Isa. 61:1-3). Moses poured the oil on his brother's head, which meant it ran down his beard and therefore bathed all the stones on the breastplate. What a beautiful picture of unity in the Lord! (Ps. 133:2) "Would God that all the Lord's people were prophets, and that the Lord would put His Spirit upon them!" (Num. 11:29)

Those who trust Jesus Christ as Savior and Lord have received an anointing of the Spirit of God (1 John 2:20, 27; 2 Cor. 1:21-22). John's emphasis is on the teaching ministry of the Spirit in guiding the believer into the truth of the Word of God. Paul's emphasis is on encouragement and stability: we have been anointed and sealed by the Spirit, and the Spirit is the "down payment" of future glory. If God has anointed us, sealed us, and given us a foretaste of heaven, then why should we despair or feel that He will ever desert us?

*The priests were forgiven (Ex. 29:10-14).* A bull was slain as a sin offering (Lev. 4; 8:14-17) to atone for the sins of the priests. This sacrifice was repeated each day for a week (Ex. 29:36-37), not only for the cleansing of the priests but also for the sanctifying of the altar where the priests would be ministering. Jesus Christ is our sin offering and through Him alone we find forgiveness (Isa. 53:4-6, 12; Matt. 26:28; 2 Cor. 5:21; 1 Peter 2:24; Rev. 1:5-6).

*The priests were completely dedicated to God (Ex. 29:15-18; Lev. 8:18-21).* In the sacrifice of the burnt offering, the animal was completely given to the Lord, a picture of total dedication (Lev. 1). Our Lord gave Himself fully and without reservation, not only in His ministry before the cross, but in His willing sacrifice of Himself on the cross. The high priest and his associates were expected to devote themselves wholly to the work of the ministry and to make it the uppermost concern of their hearts. Christians today need to meditate on Romans 12:1-2 and 1 Timothy 4:15.

The story is frequently told about a British committee that was considering inviting evangelist D.L. Moody to their city for a campaign. When a pastor spoke glowingly of Moody's ministry, a member of the committee asked rather flippantly, "Why must we have Moody? Does he have a monopoly on the Holy Spirit?"

"No," replied the pastor, "but the Holy Spirit has a monopoly on him."

*The priests were marked by the blood (Ex. 29:19-22; Lev. 8:22-24).* At this point in the ordination ceremony, we would have expected Moses to offer a trespass offering (Lev. 5), but instead, he offered a ram as a peace offering, "the ram of consecration" (Ex. 29:22, NIV, "ordination"). The Hebrew word means "filling" because the priests' hands were filled with the bread and meat.

Not only did Moses sprinkle the blood on the altar and upon Aaron and his sons, along with the anointing oil, but each man was marked with some of the blood on the right earlobe, the right thumb, and the right big toe. This was a token reminder that they must listen to God's Word, do God's work, and walk in God's way. The blood speaks of sacrifice, so the priests became "living sacrifices" in the service of the Lord (Rom. 12:1).

*The priests were fed (Ex. 29:22-28, 31-34; Lev. 8:25-29).* Another unique occurrence was the filling of the priests' hands from the "food basket" (Ex. 29:2-3) and from the altar (vv. 22-28). The priests waved these gifts toward the altar in dedication to God (v. 24, the "wave offering") and then shared them in a fellowship meal (vv. 31-34). Portions from some of the offerings, as well as special tithes of the harvest, were part of the priests' compensation for serving at the altar (Lev. 8:28-36), but they had to look upon those gifts as holy sacrifices and eat them in the tabernacle precincts.

If the priests were faithful in teaching the Word and encouraging Israel to obey the Lord, they would never lack for sustenance, for the people would be sensitive to God's Word, bring the required sacrifices and offerings to the tabernacle, and thereby provide for God's servants. It's unfortunate that some of the priests in later years were selfish and carnal and took the best for themselves (1 Sam. 2:12-17; Mal. 1:6-14).

## 5. Priests must minister daily (Ex. 29:38-46)
During the week of ordination ceremonies, the priests had to remain in the tabernacle precincts (Lev. 9:33-36), and when the week ended, they immediately entered into their ministry. No time for a day off or a vacation! In their work, they had to follow a daily, weekly, monthly, and yearly schedule, all of which was outlined in the Law that God gave Moses on Mt. Sinai.

Each day would begin with the priests sacrificing a lamb as a burnt offering, signifying the total dedication of the people to God, and the day ended with the offering of a second lamb as a burnt offering. That's a good example for us to follow, opening and closing the day with surrender to the Lord. With each lamb, they also presented a meal offering mixed with oil (Lev. 2:1-16; 6:14-23) and a drink offering of about a quart of wine, which was poured on the altar (Num. 15:1-13). For most meal offerings, the priests put only a token portion of the flour on the altar and used the rest in their own meals, but with the daily morning and evening sacrifices, this wasn't done. Everything was given to the Lord.

The flour and wine represented the results of the people's

labor in the fields and the vineyards. Symbolically, they were presenting the fruit of their toil to God and thanking Him for the strength to work and for food to eat (Deut. 8:6-18). The wine poured out was a picture of their lives poured out in His service (Phil. 2:17, NIV; 2 Tim. 4:6, NIV). All of this would please the Lord and He would find delight in dwelling in the tabernacle and blessing His people.

EXODUS 32-34; 40

# A Broken Heart
# and a Shining Face

In February 1879 in the Church of the Holy Trinity in
Philadelphia, the well-known Anglican minister Phillips
Brooks gave a series of lectures later published as *The
Influence of Jesus.* In his third lecture, he made this statement
about serving God:

> To be a true minister to men is always to accept
> new happiness and new distress, both of them
> forever deepening and entering into closer and
> more inseparable union with each other the
> more profound and spiritual ministry becomes.
> The man who gives himself to other men
> can never be a wholly sad man; but no
> more can he be a man of unclouded gladness.[1]

In the chapters before us, we see this principle vividly
illustrated in the life of Moses. His delight in God on the
mountaintop was interrupted by deep disappointment with
his people. It was one of the most heartbreaking experiences
in his entire career, and yet it brought out the best in him,
which is what always happens when we love God and live by
faith.

## 1. Guilt: God's people break the Law (Ex. 32:1–33:11)
At least three times during the months at Sinai, the Jewish
people had promised to obey whatever God told them to do

(19:8; 24:3, 7; and see 20:19). The Lord knew that it wasn't in their hearts to keep their promises (Deut. 5:28-29), and the tragedy of the golden calf proved Him right.

*The great sin (Ex. 32:1-6).* Moses called what they did "a great sin" (vv. 21, 30-31), and his assessment was accurate. It was a great sin because of who committed it: the nation of Israel, the chosen people of God, His special treasure. It was great because of when and where they committed it: at Mt. Sinai after they had heard God's Law declared and seen God's glory revealed. They had promised to obey God's Law, but in making a golden calf and indulging in a sensual celebration, the nation broke the first, second, and seventh commandments. It was a great sin because of what they had already experienced of the power and mercy of God: the judgments against Egypt, the deliverance at the Red Sea, the provision of food and water, and the gracious leading of God by the pillar of cloud and fire. What they did was rebel against the goodness of the Lord. It's no wonder their sin provoked God to anger (Deut. 9:7).

Why did Israel commit such an evil act at such a glorious time in their history? To begin with, they were impatient with Moses who had been on the mount with God for forty days and nights (vv. 11-12), and impatience is often the cause of impulsive actions that are sinful. Israel didn't know how to live by faith and trust God regardless of where their leader was. Whether Moses was with them or away from them, they criticized him and ignored what he had taught them.

But Aaron and the tribal leaders were to blame because they didn't immediately turn to God for help and warn the people what would happen. Aaron and Hur had authority from Moses to lead in his absence (Ex. 24:14), and though they were men who had seen God's mighty acts, they failed God and Moses. Instead of restraining the people, Aaron went along with them and gratified the desires of their sinful hearts. Later, he offered a feeble excuse and tried to blame the people (vv. 22-24), but God knew better. God was so angry that He would have killed Aaron had Moses not interceded for him (Deut. 9:20).

Israel's lust for idols was born in Egypt and still worked in their hearts (Josh. 24:14; Ezek. 20:4-9; 23:3, 8). Aaron fed that appetite by giving the people what they wanted. Much is being said these days about "meeting the felt needs of people," but here was a nation that didn't know what its needs really were. They thought they needed an idol, but what they really needed was faith in their great God who had revealed Himself so powerfully to them.[2] Israel exchanged the glory of the true and living God for the image of an animal (Ps. 106:19-23), which means they acted like the heathen nations around them (Rom. 1:22-27).[3] Many people can rise early to sin but not to pray.

*The great test (Ex. 32:7-14).* In leadership, the difficult experiences with our people either make us or break us, and Moses was about to be tested. God called Israel "your people whom you brought out of Egypt," as though the Lord were abandoning the nation to Moses, but Moses soon reminded Him that they were His people and that He had delivered them. Furthermore, God had made a covenant with their forefathers to bless them, multiply them, and give them their land (Gen. 12:1-3). Moses intended to hold God to His Word, and that's what God wanted him to do.

The Lord then took a different approach: He offered to wipe out Israel and make a new nation out of Moses' descendants.[4] A lesser man might have accepted this invitation, but not Moses. He loved his people, sinful as they were, and he wanted more than anything else to glorify the God of Israel and see Him fulfill His promises. Moses wasn't worried about his own future; he was concerned about God's reputation. What would the Egyptians say about God if they heard that the whole nation of Israel had been destroyed at Sinai?

God had a right to be angry at Israel's flagrant sin of idolatry and sensuality (Ex. 32:10-12), but Moses convinced God not to destroy Israel. In writing this account, Moses used human terms to describe divine actions, which is why he wrote in verse 14 that God "repented." The Hebrew word means "to grieve, to be sorry" (Gen. 6:6; 1 Sam. 15:29) and describes God's change of approach in dealing with His people (Jer. 18:1-12; 19; 26). God's character doesn't change, but God does respond to the prayers and confessions of His people.

*The great discipline (Ex. 32:15–33:11).* God in His grace forgives our sins, but God in His government allows sin to work out its terrible consequences in human life. We reap what we sow (Gal. 6:7-8). For example, God put away David's sin, but warned him that the sword wouldn't depart from his own household, and it didn't (2 Sam. 12:1-14). What a tragedy it is to reap the consequences of forgiven sin!

*Moses disciplined the people (Ex. 32:15-29).* As he came down the mountain, he asked Joshua to join him (24:12-13). One day Joshua would replace Moses, so he needed to learn how to handle these difficult matters. Moses was angry (32:19, 22), but it was anger tempered by love, which is anguish. The breaking of the stone tablets was a symbolic act: Israel had broken the covenant and would have to face discipline. But before he dealt with the people, Moses confronted Aaron, for the privilege of leadership brings with it both responsibility and accountability. Evangelist Billy Sunday said that an excuse was the skin of a reason stuffed with a lie, and Aaron's feeble excuses didn't convince Moses.

Then Moses turned to the people and asked, "Who is on the Lord's side?" (See Josh. 24:15 and 1 Kings 18:21.) This was an opportunity for all Israel to repent and reaffirm their commitment to the Lord, but only the Levites responded to the call. Ignoring the ties of family and friendship (Matt. 10:34-39; Luke 14:26-27), they courageously killed all who were involved in the orgy, which was about 3,000 men. Centuries later, Paul used this event among others to warn Christian believers about rebelling against God (1 Cor. 10:1-12).

Moses then destroyed the shameful golden calf by burning it (it may have been made of wood overlaid with gold), grinding the gold to powder, throwing the powder in a nearby stream (Ex. 17:10), and making the people drink it (Deut. 9:21).[5] By doing this he totally destroyed the idol and also forced the people to identify with their terrible sins.

Moses returned to God on Mt. Sinai where for forty more days and nights he fasted and prayed for his people (Ex. 32:30-34; 34:28; Deut. 9:18-20). He told God he was willing to be killed if it would mean life for the Jews, but God rejected his offer.[6] The Lord assured Moses that His angel would go before them and that Moses was to lead the people just as before. However, God would punish them in His own way and His own time. Had the Jews known all that Moses endured for their sake, they might have appreciated him more, but such is the price of faithful spiritual leadership.

*God disciplined the people (Ex. 32:35–33:11).* God's first discipline was to send a plague among the people, but we aren't told how many were killed. The Levites had killed 3,000 men who were engaged in idolatrous worship and immoral practices, but God knew who all the guilty people were. Sometimes God passes the sentence of judgment immediately but then delays executing the penalty. However, whether in the Old Testament or the New, "there is a sin leading to death" (1 John 5:16-17, NKJV).

God's second judgment was to refuse to go before Israel as they marched to the Promised Land (Ex. 33:1-6). God would keep the covenant promises He had made to the patriarchs, but instead of going before Israel in the person of His Son, the Angel of the Lord (23:20-23), He would appoint an angel to accompany the Jews. The reason? "You are a stiff-necked people" (32:9; 33:3, 5). If they had been a people who were suffering and afflicted, the Lord would have come to them in grace and mercy (3:7-10), but a stubborn people can only be disciplined. Better that God depart from them than that He come suddenly upon them and destroy them!

When Moses gave Israel this message, they responded by taking off their ornaments and mourning. Whether this was true repentance or not, only the Lord knew. Previously, they had contributed their gold ornaments to the making of an idol, and this had been their undoing. Perhaps they were starting to learn their lesson—the hard way.

The third judgment was to move Moses' "tent of meeting" to a site outside the camp, where he would personally meet with God. This isn't the tabernacle of the Lord, since the tabernacle had not yet been erected and dedicated. This was a special tent that Moses used when he wanted to consult with God. God graciously met with Moses and spoke with him face-to-face, the way friends talk together (Num. 12:1-8; Deut. 34:10). The cloudy pillar that led the nation on their journey would hover at the tent door, and the people would know that Moses and the Lord were in conference.

Sin is always costly, and Israel's sin had not only led to the death of thousands of people, but it had robbed the nation of the presence of the Lord in the camp and on their pilgrim journey to the Promised Land. As Charles Spurgeon said, "God never permits His people to sin successfully."

## 2. Grace: God's servant intercedes (Ex. 33:12–34:28)

During the second period of forty days and nights with God on Mt. Sinai, Moses pled for the people and asked the Lord to restore His promised blessings to them.

*God's presence with the nation (Ex. 33:12-17).* Moses reminded the Lord of His promise to accompany the people on their journey. In fact, when the nation sang God's praises at the Red Sea, they rejoiced in the promise of God's victorious presence (15:13-18). Was God now going to go back on His Word?

Moses based his appeal on the grace (favor) of God, for he knew that the Lord was merciful and gracious and that the people were guilty. If God gave them what they deserved, they would have been destroyed! The Jews were God's people and Moses was God's servant. They didn't want an angel to accompany them, for there was nothing special about that. The thing that distinguished Israel from the other nations was that their God was present with them, and that's what Moses requested. His heart must have leaped for joy when he heard God promise to accompany the people and lead them to the place of rest that He had promised.

Do God's children have the right to "negotiate" with God as Moses did? It all depends on our relationship with God. Moses knew the ways of God (Ps. 103:7) and was the intimate friend of God, and therefore he was able to present his case with faith and skill. The godly Scottish minister Samuel Rutherford, who knew what it was to suffer for Christ, wrote, "It is faith's work to claim and challenge loving-kindness out of all the roughest strokes of God." That's what Moses was doing for the people.

*God's glory revealed (Ex. 33:18-23).* The true servant of God is concerned more about the glory of God than about anything else. Moses and the Jews had seen God's glory in the pillar of cloud and fire, as well as in the "storm" on Mt. Sinai, but Moses wanted to see the intimate glory of God revealed to him personally. God did give Moses a guarded glimpse of His glory and he was satisfied. When God's servants are discouraged and disappointed because of the sins of their people, the best remedy for a broken heart is a new vision of the glory of God.

*God's forgiveness granted (Ex. 34:1-28).* Moses had won God's promise to accompany the people in their journey, but would He forgive the people for their sins? Would He accompany them like a policeman watching a criminal or like a Father caring for His beloved children? The answer came when the Lord ordered Moses to prepare two new stone tablets, for this meant He was going to replace the tablets that Moses had broken! God would renew the covenant! Early the next morning, Moses kept the appointment, the tablets in his hands.

But before He did anything with the tablets, God proclaimed the greatness of His attributes (vv. 5-7), a declaration that is basic to all Jewish and Christian theology. Moses repeated these words to God at Kadesh-Barnea (Num. 14:17-19), the Jews used them in Nehemiah's day (Neh. 9:17-18), and Jonah quoted them when he sat pouting outside Nineveh (Jonah 4:1-2). We don't read that Moses fell on his face when he saw the glimpses of God's glory, but he did bow to the ground and worship when he heard God speak these magnificent words.

Faith comes by hearing and receiving God's Word (Rom. 10:17), so Moses by faith asked God to forgive the people. The pronouns in this prayer are significant: "pardon *our* iniquity and *our* sin" (Ex. 33:9, italics mine). Though he wasn't guilty of disobeying God, Moses identified himself with the sins of the people, as did Ezra and Daniel in their prayers of confession (Ezra 9; Dan. 9). The Lord had just declared that He forgave "iniquity and transgression and sin" (Ex. 33:7), and Moses laid hold of that truth.

The fact that God renewed the covenant is evidence that He forgave His people and gave them a new beginning. But God also repeated the essential elements of the covenant, especially the laws about idolatry (vv. 12-17). When Israel moved into their Promised Land, it would be very easy to compromise with the enemy, first by making agreements with them, then by joining in their feasts, and finally by intermarrying with them and adopting their pagan ways. It was important from the very beginning that Israel repudiate and destroy everything associated with idols and to realize that what adultery was to marriage, idolatry was to their covenant with the Lord.

We who live many millennia after these events can't begin to comprehend how filthy Canaanite idolatry was when Israel conquered the land. It was unspeakably immoral, and like cancerous tumors in human bodies, the pagan temples and altars had to be removed and destroyed before the land could be healthy. God had called Israel to be the channel of blessing to the world, culminating in the birth of the Savior, and idolatry was the enemy that almost destroyed the nation. Humanly speaking, were it not for a faithful remnant after the Captivity that struggled to be true to God, the world might not have had the written Scriptures and the birth of the Savior.

By the grace of God, Moses achieved his purposes: God promised to go with the people, God showed Moses a glimpse of His glory, and God forgave the sins of the nation. Moses could return to the camp with the second tables of the Law and tell the people God had forgiven their sins.

### 3. Glory: God's presence dwells with the people (Ex. 34:29-35; 39:32–40:38)

The Book of Exodus opens with Moses seeing God's glory in the burning bush (3:1-5), and it closes with the glory of God descending into the camp and filling the tabernacle. The presence of the glory of God in the camp of Israel was not a luxury; it was a necessity. It identified Israel as the people of

God and set them apart from the other nations, for the tabernacle was consecrated by the glory of God (29:43-44). Other nations had sacred buildings, but they were empty. The tabernacle of Israel was blessed with the presence of the glory of God.

*God's glory reflected (Ex. 34:29-35; 2 Cor. 3).* Moses had been fasting and praying in the presence of God for eighty days, and he had seen a glimpse of God's glory. Is it any wonder that he had a shining face? He didn't realize that he had "absorbed" some of the glory and was reflecting it from his countenance.[7] Because of this glory, the people were afraid to come near him, but he summoned them to come and they talked as before. However, after he was finished speaking to the people, Moses put on a veil to cover the glory.

Why did Moses wear a veil? Not because he was frightening the people, but because the glory was fading away (2 Cor. 3:13). The Jews saw this glory as something wonderful and exciting, but what would they say if they knew it was fading away? Who wants to follow a leader who is losing his glory? So Moses would go into the tent of meeting to talk with God, and the glory would return, but then he would wear the veil so the people wouldn't see the glory disappear.

In 2 Corinthians 3, Paul made several applications of this remarkable event. First, he pointed out that the glory of the Mosaic legal system was fading away, but that the glory of the Gospel of God's grace was getting more glorious (vv. 7-11). This was his answer to the legalists who taught that obedience to the Law *plus* faith in Christ was God's way of salvation (Acts 15:1). Why believe in something when its glory is vanishing?

He also applied the event to the lost Jews of his day whose hearts were covered by a veil of unbelief so they couldn't see the glory of Christ (2 Cor. 3:14-16). The only way to remove that veil was to believe the Word and trust in Jesus Christ.

Finally, he applied Moses' experience to Christians who by faith see the glory of Jesus Christ in the Word and experience a spiritual transformation (vv. 17-18). This is why Christians read the Bible and meditate on it, because when the child of God looks into the Word of God and sees the Son of God, he or she is transformed by the Spirit of God into the image of God for the glory of God.[8]

*God's glory resident (Ex. 39:32–40:38).* The people of Israel had no idea what Moses had experienced on the mountain and how close they had come to being rejected by God and destroyed. Never underestimate the spiritual power of a dedicated man or woman who knows how to intercede with God. One of our greatest needs today is for intercessors who can lay hold of God's promises and trust God to work in mighty power (Isa. 59:16; 62:1; 64:1-7).

The work on the tabernacle and its furnishings was now completed, so the workers brought it all to Moses for his inspection. It would have been foolish to erect the tabernacle and put the furnishings and utensils in place only to discover that the workers had made serious mistakes. The word "commanded" is used eighteen times in Exodus 39 and 40 to remind us that the workers did what God had told them to do. Moses was a faithful servant who did all that God told him to do (Heb. 3:1-6).

The work was approved and the building was constructed (Ex. 40:1-8, 17-19, 33). This chapter summarizes the dedication of the priests, which was already described in Exodus 28–29, as well as the dedication of the building and its contents. Moses personally saw to it that every piece of furniture and every utensil was anointed and placed where it ought to be. God could not and would not dwell in the tabernacle unless everything was done according to the pattern He showed Moses on the mount (25:8-9, 40; Heb. 8:5; 9:9).[9]

Too many sincere people have tried to do God's work their

own way and then have asked God to bless it. But ministry doesn't work that way. First we find out what God wants us to do, and we do it to glorify Him. If we obey His will and seek to honor His name, then He will come and bless the work with His powerful presence.

After everything and everybody associated with the tabernacle was dedicated to the Lord, then the glory of God filled the tabernacle and abode there. The Hebrew word translated "abode" in Exodus 39:35 ("settled," NIV) is transliterated *shekinah* in English, "the abiding presence of God." (See 24:16 and 25:8.) So powerful was the presence of God's glory that Moses wasn't able to enter the tabernacle!

When you read Jewish history, you discover that the glory that once dwelt in the tabernacle departed from it when the priests and the people sinned against the Lord (1 Sam. 4:21-22). Ichabod means "the glory is gone." When Solomon dedicated the temple, God's glory once again came to dwell with His people (1 Kings 8:10-11), but once again their sins drove God's glory away (Ezek. 8:4; 9:3; 10:4, 18; 11:23).

The next time the glory of God came to earth was in the person of Jesus Christ (John 1:14). In the Greek translation of the Old Testament (the Septuagint), the word "abode" in Exodus 39:35 is the Greek word used in Luke 1:35 and translated "overshadowed." Mary's virgin womb was a holy of holies where the glory of God dwelt in the person of God's Son. What did the world do with this glory? Nailed it to a cross!

Where is God's glory today? The body of every true believer is the temple of God (1 Cor. 6:19-20), but so is the local church (3:10-23) and the church universal (Eph. 2:20-22). When Solomon finished the temple, the glory of God moved in, but when God finishes building His church, He will move the church out! Then we will share God's glory in heaven for all eternity! "And the city had no need of the sun or of the moon to shine in it, for the glory of God illuminated it, and the Lamb is its light" (Rev. 21:22, NKJV).

God today doesn't live in buildings (Acts 7:48-50; 1 Kings 8:7). Buildings are dedicated to God to be used as tools for His work and His workers. But God does dwell in His people, and it's our responsibility to glorify God individually (1 Cor. 6:20) and collectively (14:23-25). What a tragedy it would be if the glory departed and we had to write "Ichabod" on our buildings. How much better it would be if, like Moses, we did everything according to the heavenly pattern so that God's glory would feel at home in our midst.

# AFTERWORD

As we've studied Exodus, we've traveled with Moses from the glory of God in the burning bush to the glory of God in the tabernacle. What are the basic truths we've learned?

1. God's purpose for His people is freedom. He doesn't want us to be in bondage to self, sin, or the world.

2. God's purpose in freedom is that His people manifest responsible conduct and service. Freedom isn't the privilege of doing whatever we want to do. It's the opportunity to do whatever God wants us to do.

3. Responsible freedom (maturity) comes as we experience trials and testings and trust God to see us through. Complaining when life becomes difficult is a mark of spiritual immaturity.

4. God wants to dwell with us in a deeper way (John 14:21-24). Our sins grieve Him and He withdraws His fellowship and blessing when we rebel. We have a heavenly Intercessor and Advocate in Jesus Christ, and we can confess our sins to Him and be forgiven (1 John 1:5–2:2).

5. Believers today are a kingdom of priests whose first responsibility is to worship and please God. Everything we are and everything we do depends on that. As priests, we must minister to one another and to a lost world.

6. The most important goal in the Christian life is to be able to stand before God one day and say sincerely, "I have glorified You on the earth. I have finished the work which You have given me to do" (John 17:4, NKJV).

BE DELIVERED

## Chapter One
*Wanted: A Deliverer*
(Exodus 1–4)

1. What is the definition of freedom? How can freedom be misused? How should it be properly used?

2. What special tasks did God give Israel to accomplish on the earth?

3. What steps did Pharaoh take to control the Jewish people?

4. The Israelite midwives disobeyed Pharaoh's command to kill the Jewish baby boys. When, if ever, is civil disobedience the right choice? Why?

5. What did God use to equip Moses? What in your life might God be using to equip you for service?

6. How did Moses get transformed from a compassionate but impetuous leader into one called "the meekest man on earth"? What was the key difference?

7. What five reasons did Moses give for not accepting God's call? If you heard a call from God to ministry, which reason(s) would you likely use to dodge the call?

8. What is true humility?

9. What five encouragements did God give to Moses as he stepped out in faith?

10. Having Aaron along was an encouragement to Moses. Who is an encouragement to you as you serve the Lord? How can you be an encouragement to someone with whom you serve?

## Chapter Two

### *War Is Declared*
(Exodus 5:1–8:19)

1. Why was it reasonable for Pharaoh to ask, "Why should I obey the Lord?"

2. Why did the Israelites turn against Moses and Aaron so quickly? What couldn't they see?

3. What two sins characterized the people of Israel during the Exodus and the next forty years? Why are these such common sins among God's people?

4. What must Christian leaders do when they encounter opposition and misunderstanding? What is usually your first response?

5. How does Wiersbe say we can experience peace in the tough times?

6. Why did God take the approach of using sign judgments with Pharaoh?

7. In what ways were the plagues a judgment not only on the Egyptians but also their gods?

8. What does it mean that Pharaoh hardened his heart?

9. Why can God still hold Pharaoh responsible for his hard heart when God at times was described as doing the hardening?

10. When have you, like Pharaoh, made a promise to God in times of trouble but then did not follow through?

# Chapter Three
## *"The Lord, Mighty in Battle"*
(Exodus 8:20–10:29)

1. Why do you think God didn't send His judgment in one terrible blow when freeing the Israelites from Egypt?

2. How was God's providential care for the Israelites seen in the last seven plagues?

3. What do you learn about God through the various plagues?

4. What were God's purposes in the plagues?

5. What is the opposite of a hard heart? What does this mean?

6. How, if at all, can a hard heart be softened?

7. Pharaoh confessed his sin but then proved to be insincere. What are the marks of a sincere confession?

8. How can a family or a church pass on to the young people the wonders God has worked in previous generations?

9. Why did Moses and Aaron reject the offer for all the people, but no flocks and herds, to go on the journey?

10. In what way is the hardening of Pharaoh's heart a warning to all of us?

## Chapter Four

### *One More Plague*
(Exodus 11:1–13:16)

1. Wiersbe asks two questions about the last plague: (1) Why did God slay the firstborn? (2) Was He just in doing so when Pharaoh was the true culprit?

2. God often rejected the firstborn son as the special one. What does this rejection symbolize?

3. What or who does the Passover lamb picture? How do you know this?

4. What did the Jews need to do with the Passover lamb in order to be saved?

5. How does this Passover action symbolize our own salvation?

6. What is the spiritual significance of each aspect of the Passover meal: roasted lamb, unleavened bread, and bitter herbs?

7. What is the yeast an image of? What other Scripture passages use yeast as an example?

8. How are the Passover meal and the Lord's Supper similar?

9. What might distinguish a true child of God from one of the "mixed multitude"?

10. What is faith? How did Moses exercise his faith in the Lord?

## Chapter Five

### *Redeemed and Rejoicing*
(Exodus 13:17-15:21)

1. What, according to Charles Kingsley, is the difference between false and true freedom?

2. What were Israel's three important responsibilities after they were set free?

3. The Israelites were saved from bondage in Egypt to freedom in the Promised Land. What are you saved from and what are you saved to?

4. How did God visibly guide the Israelites to the Red Sea? How does God guide believers today?

5. When did the Israelites become frightened and begin to complain? What did they forget?

6. What works of the Lord have you heard of or seen that will help you to believe and trust in God in times of trial?

7. Why, in view of the Israelites' complaining and lack of faith, did God perform the miracles of the Exodus?

8. What must genuine faith depend on? What must it not depend on?

9. What two ingredients of true worship do we see in the celebration and praise hymn after the Red Sea crossing?

10. As the Israelites entered the wilderness, what did their song of victory and praise turn into? What changed?

STUDY QUESTIONS

## Chapter Six

# The School of Life
(Exodus 15:22–16:36)

1. What four important truths does Wiersbe draw out from the activities of the Israelites in the Book of Exodus?

2. What challenging experiences are you now facing that will hopefully help you to mature and glorify God?

3. What is the difference between the Lord's testing and the devil's tempting?

4. How can people "tempt" God?

5. What is the right response when facing a problem? In what different ways might God answer a cry for help?

6. The Israelites remembered the good but not the hardship of Egypt. How can believers keep a proper perspective about the past and the present?

7. What does it mean to "live on promises and not explanations"?

8. What spiritual lessons can be learned from God's provision of the manna?

9. Where might God be testing you for obedience like He tested the Israelites with the manna instructions?

10. How can you be sure to remember a spiritual lesson the Lord taught you?

## Chapter Seven
# *"The Lord of Hosts Is with Us"*
### (Exodus 17-18)

1. God promises that He will be with you always, as He was with Moses. How does this change your experience of daily life?

2. Why was God leading Israel into difficult situations?

3. In the second test of lack of water, what blocked Israel from applying what they had learned the first time?

4. What did Moses need to do again and again in his frustrating task of leadership?

5. What place along your life's journey could sadly be called "Massah" and "Meribah"? How could you have responded better in that place?

6. Why does Wiersbe say Moses got weary while holding up the rod of God?

7. Aaron and Hur played crucial supporting roles in the victories of Israel. How can you be a support and share in the battle through your local church?

8. How can you incorporate more times of praise in your relationship with the Lord?

9. Who did God use to help Moses be a more effective leader? Why was this surprising?

10. What does Moses' adjustment of the leadership structure teach the church about ministry?

## Chapter Eight

### *Hear the Voice of God*
(Exodus 19:1–20:21)

1. God told the Israelites that He bore them on eagles' wings. What does this mean? What does Wiersbe say eagles and eaglets have to teach us about the life of maturity and freedom?

2. What has been your most recent "turning point" in life? What new freedoms, privileges, and responsibilities came with it?

3. What does it mean that the Jews are God's chosen people, His treasured possession? Where does that leave the other nations?

4. In which areas or activities of life were the Israelites to be holy, set apart, or different? How are believers today to be set apart?

5. Why couldn't the people (besides Moses) touch Mt. Sinai? What was God teaching them?

6. What was the purpose(s) of the giving of the Ten Commandments?

7. In the Ten Commandments, what is the significance of the repeated phrase "the Lord thy God"?

8. What is an idol? What other religions include idol worship? What are some less obvious idols that entice us today?

9. What do the first and the tenth commandments have in common?

10. In what way is love the fulfillment of the Law?

# Chapter Nine

## *The Book of the Covenant*
### (Exodus 20:22–24:8)

1. What are the laws of God based upon?

2. What can the Law do, and what can it not do?

3. What are some differences between the religion of the one true God and the false religions?

4. How can we ensure that our enthusiastic promises are followed up by obedience?

5. What is true justice?

6. In Exodus 21:15, 18, God ordered the death penalty for striking or cursing parents. What principle can a Christian parent learn from this? What would be an appropriate consequence of such sins today?

7. As we read biblical passages dealing with specific laws governing the everyday affairs of Israel, how, if at all, do we make personal application?

8. How do you understand the Old Testament justice of "an eye for an eye" alongside Jesus' teaching of "turn the other cheek"? (See Matt. 5:38-39.)

9. What does it take for an offender to make things right?

10. What was required of the Israelites to receive God's blessing?

## Chapter Ten

# The Place Where God Dwells— Part I

(Exodus 24:9–25:40; 27:20-21;
30:11-16; 31:1-11; 35:4–36:38;
37:1-24; 38:21-31)

1. Since even the highest heavens cannot contain God, what does it mean that God came to dwell with His people?

2. Amid all the details for building the tabernacle, what else is taught?

3. How does God describe His distance from the Israelites and from believers in the Christian era?

4. How does the spiritual lesson, "God provides the material," encourage you today?

5. How are Christians, like Bezalel and Oholiah, equipped and enabled for service?

6. What does the ark of the covenant represent and what does it teach?

7. What was the significance of the twelve loaves in the holy place?

8. How do prayer, the Word, and the Holy Spirit work together?

9. What is the most important part of a Christian's life?

10. What are the dangers of overemphasizing either the transcendence or immanence of God?

## Chapter Eleven

# *The Place Where God Dwells— Part II*

(Exodus 26:1-37; 27:1-19; 30:1-10, 17-21; 37:25-29; 38:1-20)

1. What does the burning of incense picture?

2. What must true prayer be based on?

3. The ingredients for incense were a prescribed mixture of spices. What are some of the ingredients of prayer? Which are you most in danger of neglecting?

4. What was the significance of salting the incense?

5. What might the brazen altar symbolize? What has taken the place of the brazen altar today?

6. What is the only altar believers now have? What do we present there?

7. What does the water for drinking and the water for washing symbolize? What then does the laver typify?

8. What importance does Wiersbe see in the different colors used in the tabernacle?

9. Where in the New Testament is the "veil" mentioned?

10. What is food and drink to a believer's soul? How can our hunger and thirst be increased?

STUDY QUESTIONS

## Chapter Twelve
*The Holy Priesthood*
(Exodus 28–29; 30:22-33; 39)

1. What was the first obligation of the priests? What is the first obligation of God's people today?

2. What was important about the design of the ephod? How can believers spiritually wear the ephod?

3. From studying the breastplate of the high priest, what can be learned about ministry in the church?

4. Why did the high priest carry the Urim and Thummim?

5. How can we know what, if anything, is symbolized by these Old Testament details?

6. What does Wiersbe say is the first step to happiness? Why would unbelievers think this is ridiculous?

7. What does it mean to fear the Lord? What is a mistaken understanding of this?

8. The cleansing of the hands and feet at the laver was a type of what other kind of cleansing?

9. Who has been anointed with the Spirit of God? What is gained from the anointing?

10. What does it mean for believers to "present your bodies as a living and holy sacrifice"? (Rom. 12:1)

## Chapter Thirteen

# A Broken Heart and a Shining Face
(Exodus 32-34; 40)

1. Why was the making of the golden calf such a great sin? What led up to this grievous action?

2. What should the leaders have done when approached with the request for an idol?

3. Why is it not always a good thing to meet the "felt needs" of people?

4. What does it mean that God "repented" or "changed His mind"? (32:14)

5. Why did God record the history of Israel's relationship with God? (See 1 Cor. 10:11-13.)

6. How can a person know if something is a discipline from the Lord or not?

7. In what manner have you glimpsed the glory of God?

8. In the great declaration of His attributes, God proclaims that He will "by no means leave the guilty unpunished." What does this mean?

9. How did Paul apply the event of Moses wearing a veil over his face?

10. How should believers plan for ministry without being presumptuous?

# NOTES

**Chapter 1**

1. There are fourteen Old Testament books that begin with "and" in the original text: Exodus, Leviticus, Joshua, Judges, Ruth, 1 and 2 Samuel, 1 and 2 Kings, 2 Chronicles, Ezra, Esther, Ezekiel, and Jonah. Most English translations either ignore the "and" or translate it "now."

2. See my book *Be Authentic* (Chariot Victor) for an exposition of the life of Joseph and the last days of Jacob. The Hebrew word translated "name" is *shem*, and Shem was the son of Noah through whom the Hebrew nation came (Gen. 11:10).

3. Exodus 1:9 is the first instance in the Bible of the phrase "the Children of Israel."

4. The word "Hyksos" means "rulers of foreign countries." The Hyksos were outsiders who infiltrated Egypt as servants and slaves and gradually took over the government, ruling during the fifteenth and sixteenth dynasties (1700–1542 B.C.). Being Semitic in origin, they would certainly identify with the Jews living in Egypt.

5. With so many Jewish women bearing so many children, it's likely that Shiphrah and Puah were "chief midwives" and had other women working under their supervision. The Egyptians were masters of organization and probably had a Bureau of Resident Alien Obstetrics.

6. These examples teach us that when Christians disobey the law because of conscience, their decisions must be based on the clear laws of God found in Scripture and not simply on personal prejudice. Note too that the midwives, Daniel and his friends, and the apostles were courteous in the way they dealt with the civil authorities and used the experience to bear witness of the truth of God. Jesus is the

supreme example (1 Peter 2:13-25).

7. God's law is clear that it's wrong both to murder and to lie, but there are times in this evil world when we may have to choose between greater and lesser evils, and we need the wisdom of God to direct us (James 1:5). The legalist simply obeys the letter of the law, and the pragmatist does what seems safe and right at the time, but the spiritually minded person seeks the mind of Christ. As long as this world is in the travail of sin (Rom. 8:22), we will face difficult decisions.

8. Many conservative Bible scholars date the Exodus at about 1445 B.C. If Moses was eighty years old at the time of the Exodus (Ex. 7:7), then he was born about 1525 B.C.

9. Both Acts 7:20 and Hebrews 11:23 literally read "fair in the sight of God." Since the parents acted by faith, and faith comes through the Word (Rom. 10:17), Amram and Jochebed must have had some communication from the Lord that Moses was special to Him.

10. We shouldn't infer from the word "pleasures" that Moses was enjoying carnal delights in the palace. Rather, it was the pleasure enjoyed by a successful man of position. As a prince and "a man mighty in words and deeds," he had authority, respect, and security and needed nothing.

11. The name Gershom means "alien, stranger." Stephen points out in Acts 7:13, 35-36 that, like Jesus, both Joseph and Moses were rejected by their brethren at their first encounter but accepted at the second. Also, like Jesus, each man took a bride during the period of alienation from his people.

12. In Numbers 10:29 you find Raguel as an alternate spelling of Reuel and learn that his son's name was Hobab. However, Judges 4:11 names Hobab as the "father-in-law of Moses." The Hebrew word means "a husband's male relative by marriage" and can refer to either a brother-in-law or a father-in-law and should be translated "brother-in-law."

13. God's promises to Abraham had been passed down from generation to generation, so that Moses would be able to connect God's words in Exodus 3:18 with the promises in Genesis 15:13-21. It was all part of God's "continued story" of redemption.

14. The older versions of the Bible transliterate the Hebrew name for God as "Jehovah," but modern scholars prefer "Yahweh."

15. In Egypt, Moses had been "mighty in word" (Acts 7:22), but his years of shepherding seemed to have silenced him.

## Chapter 2

1. *The Works of Jonathan Edwards,* Banner of Truth Trust edition, 1976; vol. 2, p. 10. This is probably the most famous, least read, and most criticized sermon ever preached in America. Edwards preached it at Enfield, Massachusetts, on July 8, 1741, and God used it to begin a powerful spiritual awakening in New England.

2. Many scholars believe that the Pharaoh of the Exodus was Amenhotep II, son of Thutmose III, the Pharaoh of the oppression, whose death opened the way for Moses to return to Egypt.

3. "Let My people go" is found seven times in the pre-Exodus narrative: 5:1; 7:16; 8:1, 20; 9:1, 13; 10:3.

4. The Lord had promised that the nation would worship Him at Mt. Sinai (3:12), but they could never reach Sinai in three days (19:1). However, Moses knew that Pharaoh wouldn't let the people go (3:12-22); therefore, his words, though sincere, were but the first "volley" in God's war against Pharaoh. God's command gave Pharaoh an opportunity either to submit to the Lord or to reveal the sinfulness of his own proud heart.

5. God reminded the Jews that He was Jehovah (6:2, 6-8,

29; 10:2; 16:12; 20:2; 29:46; 31:13), but He also wanted the Egyptians to know that He was the Lord (7:5, 17; 8:22; 14:4, 18). The name "Jehovah" is translated as LORD (all capitals) in most English translations of the Bible. It is used 6,823 times in the Old Testament.

6. See Genesis 17:1; 28:3; 35:11; 43:14; 48:3; 49:3. "El Shaddai" (God Almighty) is used thirty times in the Book of Job and eight times in the Book of Revelation. Both of these books emphasize the greatness of God's power.

7. The first nine plagues divide into three triads, each triad climaxing with a plague that wasn't announced. The third (gnats), sixth (boils), and ninth (darkness) plagues came without warning; all the others were preceded by an announcement. Pharaoh had no right to complain because God told him what He was going to do.

8. The fact that there were still frogs in the river indicates that the water was again normal (8:11). If the water were still blood, the frogs would have died.

9. Since the Lord is holy, just, and good, and His ways are perfect, nobody has to defend what He does or try to explain why He does it (Rom. 9:14-21). God gave Pharaoh many opportunities to repent and yet he hardened his heart by the way he responded to God's clear revelation of Himself. What more could Moses and Aaron have done?

10. The Hebrew word is translated "lice" in the KJV and NKJV, and "gnats" in the NIV and NASB. Some scholars think it might have been a plague of mosquitoes. God sent swarms of little, flying, biting creatures that made life miserable for the Egyptians.

## Chapter 3
1. Pharaoh had given the land of Goshen to Joseph's family in appreciation for all Joseph had done for the land of Egypt. See Genesis 45:10 and 50:8.

2. See Exodus 19:5-6 and Deuteronomy 32:8-9; 33:16. Balaam recognized the distinctiveness of Israel as a nation when he called the Jews "a people who live apart and do not consider themselves one of the nations" (Num. 23:9, NIV). In Romans 9:1-5, Paul lists the special blessings God gave to the people of Israel. The fact that the Jews are God's chosen people doesn't mean they're better than any other people (Deut. 7:6-11) but that they belong to God in a special way, have special tasks to perform in this world, and are held accountable in a special way because of these privileges (Amos 3:2).

3. The goddess Hathor was pictured having the head of a cow, the god Apis the head of a bull, and Khnum the head of a ram. The cow was sacred to Isis and the ram to Amon. If the Egyptians had seen the Israelites sacrificing these animals to Jehovah, they would have protested violently and probably attacked the Jews who, after all, were nothing but slaves in the land.

4. Inasmuch as there were still livestock in Egypt that were affected by the next two plagues (9:9, 19-21), the word "all" in verse 6 should be interpreted in a relative sense. Note too that the livestock killed by the fifth plague were in the fields, not in sheds (vv. 19-21).

5. God warned Israel that if they disobeyed Him after entering the Promised Land, He would send them the same painful boils with which He had afflicted the Egyptians (Deut. 28:27, 35).

6. The fact that God allowed Pharaoh to be the ruler of Egypt, was long-suffering toward him, and mercifully spared his life, doesn't imply that God was to blame for Pharaoh's decisions. When God isn't allowed to rule, then He overrules and always accomplishes His purposes. However, He doesn't deprive people of the privilege of choice nor does He deny human responsibility. The Jews couldn't blame God for what Pharaoh did, nor could Pharaoh absolve himself of responsi-

bility.

7. The Jews considered thunder to be the voice of God (Ps. 29; John 12:29), and thunder often accompanied the great works of God (Ex. 19:19; 20:18; 1 Sam. 7:10; 12:17).

8. Pharaoh is one of six people in Scripture who said, "I have sinned" but gave no evidence of true repentance: Balaam (Num. 22:34), Achan (Josh. 7:20), King Saul (1 Sam. 15:24, 30; 26:21), Shimei (2 Sam. 19:20), and Judas (Matt. 27:4). Those who said it and proved their repentance by their obedience were David (2 Sam. 12:13; 24:10, 17; 1 Chron. 21:8, 17; Ps. 51:4) and the prodigal son (Luke 15:18, 21).

9. It is this incident that is referred to in Hebrews 11:27. Moses wasn't afraid of the wrath of Pharaoh as he organized the Jewish people and led them out of Egypt, for he knew that God would defeat Pharaoh and his army.

10. The parallels between the plagues of Egypt and the judgments in the Book of Revelation are worth noting: water turned to blood (8:8; 16:4-6), frogs (16:13), painful sores (16:2), hail and fire (8:7), locusts (9:1), and terrible darkness (16:10).

**Chapter 4**

1. The phrase "all the congregation of Israel" (v. 3) is found here for the first time in the Bible and indicates that God was now looking upon His people as one nation. Passover united the people around the killing of the Lamb (12:6), the putting away of the leaven (v. 19), and the eating of the feast (v. 47). See also 16:1-2, 9-10, 22 and 17:1.

2. In the Book of Revelation, Jesus Christ is called "the Lamb" twenty-eight times, and the Greek word used means "a little pet lamb." God's judgment is "the wrath of the Lamb" (6:16); the bride is "the wife of the Lamb" (21:9); and the throne is "the throne of the Lamb" (22:1, 3). The lamb is a type of Jesus Christ because the New Testament makes this

clear. That is the ultimate and important mark of a type. Not everything that people call "types" of Christ really meet the New Testament qualification.

3. Keep in mind that the Jewish day was reckoned from evening to evening. The Passover lamb was slain "between the evenings" on Friday the fourteenth of Nisan, before the arrival of the next day. Israel left Egypt on the fifteenth of Nisan, at night.

4. John 6:51-59 compares our spiritual communion with Christ to feasting on Him. The literally minded Jews misunderstood this image and thought that Jesus was telling them to eat human flesh and drink blood, but He explained that He was speaking about feeding on His Word (6:63). Peter got the message and expressed it clearly (vv. 66-68). To call John 6 a sermon on the Lord's Supper (Communion, Eucharist) is to miss the point completely. Why would Jesus discuss a "family matter" like the Lord's Supper with an unbelieving Jewish crowd when He hadn't even mentioned the subject to His own disciples?

5. "And your house" in Acts 16:31 doesn't mean that the father's faith would automatically save his children, but that the children could claim the same promise as their father and be saved. However, the statement reveals God's special concern for families. He wants the children to believe and be saved.

6. This practice started about the second century before Christ. The four passages copied were Exodus 13:1-10, 11-16; Deuteronomy 6:4-9; 11:13-21. The English word "phylactery" is a transliteration of the Greek word *phulakterion* meaning "an amulet, safeguard, means of protection." It is the Greek equivalent of the Hebrew word for these little boxes—*tephillin*—which means "prayers."

7. When Israel got too friendly with the Midianites, it led to divine judgment and 24,000 people died. See Numbers 25.

**Chapter 5**

1. George Morrison, Sunrise: *Addresses from a City Pulpit* (London: Hodder and Stoughton), 66.

2. A.W. Tozer, *That Incredible Christian* (Christian Publications: 1964), 44–46.

3. If you consult more than one Bible atlas, you'll discover that Old Testament scholars don't agree on the exact route of the Exodus. For one thing, they aren't sure where some of the cities were located that are mentioned in the text (14:2). A second factor is that the Hebrew *yam suph*, usually translated "Red Sea" can also be translated "sea of reeds," that is, one of the smaller bodies of water north of Succoth. One of the best discussions is found in *The Moody Atlas of Bible Lands* by Berry J. Beitzel (Chicago: Moody Press, 1985), 85–93.

4. Starting with Genesis 15:1 and ending with Revelation 1:17, the "fear not" statements of the Bible are a profitable study.

5. In the New Testament, the word "exodus" describes our Lord's passion and work of redemption on the cross (Luke 9:31; "decease" in KJV) as well as the death and homegoing of the believer (2 Peter 1:15). Jesus saw His suffering as a "baptism" (Luke 12:50), when "all the waves and billows" of God's judgment went over Him (Ps. 42:7).

6. Some Bible students believe that Psalm 118 was sung at the laying of the foundation of the second temple, as recorded in Ezra 3:8-13. Compare verse 11 with Psalm 118:1-4, and note how the entire psalm parallels the experiences of the Jewish remnant in the land, especially verses 10-14 and verses 18-23.

7. The emphasis in Isaiah 11–12 is on the future regathering of Israel to their land and the glorious kingdom of Messiah. Isaiah 11:15 even pictures a "second exodus" and a

drying up of the sea to allow the Jews to cross. It will be a happy time for Israel, and they will sing to the Lord as they did at the Red Sea.

8. In heaven, the tribulation saints will sing "the song of Moses . . . and the song of the Lamb" (Rev. 15). Israel sang by an earthly sea, but they will sing by the heavenly "sea of glass, mingled with fire." Israel sang *after* seeing God's judgments poured out on one nation, but the heavenly saints sing *before* the angels pour out the seven bowls of wrath on the whole world. In both instances, God's power is revealed and God's name is glorified.

9. Of course, God is spirit and as such doesn't have a body, so the mentioning of His hand and His nostrils is simply figurative poetic language. Theologians call this "anthropomorphism," the use of human characteristics to describe divine attributes and actions.

10. Why Miriam is called "the sister of Aaron" rather than "Moses and Aaron" is a puzzle. Both Aaron and Miriam were older than Moses and had no doubt been together in Egypt while Moses was in Midian, and therefore were close to each other. Perhaps phrasing it like this was one way Moses had to show that his sister in her leadership was identified with Aaron the priest, perhaps as a director of praise, and not with Moses the prophet. When she and Aaron stepped out of line, God chastened them (Num. 12). This is the only place in Exodus where she is mentioned by name, although we assume it was Miriam who guarded the baby Moses (Ex. 2:1-10).

11. For other biblical prophetesses, see Judges 4:4; 2 Kings 22:14; Nehemiah 6:14; Isaiah 8:3; Luke 2:36; and Acts 21:9. In his Pentecostal sermon, Peter quoted Joel 2:28-32 and affirmed that the coming of the Spirit would enable their sons and daughters to prophesy (Acts 2:17-18). Not all Bible students agree that the gift of prophecy is still in the church,

especially now that we have the completed Word of God. The danger in the church is not false prophets but false teachers (2 Peter 2:1; 1 Tim. 4:1-2).

**Chapter 6**

1. Often after a great victory of faith, the Lord permits a trial to come to test us. When Abraham arrived in the Promised Land, he discovered a famine (Gen. 12:10), and after the glorious occasion of His baptism, our Lord was tempted by Satan in the wilderness (Matt. 3:13–4:11). Elijah won a great victory on Mt. Carmel, but after that faced a trial of faith (1 Kings 18–19).

2. This is one of several "compound names" of the Lord found in the Old Testament. See Genesis 22:13-14; Exodus 17:15; Judges 6:24; Jeremiah 23:6; Ezekiel 48:35.

3. A type is an Old Testament person, object, institution, ritual, or event that points to a spiritual truth yet to be revealed. There are many Old Testament "illustrations" of New Testament spiritual truth, but in order to be true types, those illustrations must be authorized by the New Testament. For example, the relationship between Ruth and Boaz illustrates the love between Christ and the church, but nowhere does the New Testament call this a type. The same is true of Joseph, who in many ways reminds us of Jesus Christ. Some scholars call these "inferred types" because they parallel so many New Testament truths. Besides the manna, other types of Christ include Adam (Rom. 5:14), Melchizedek (Gen. 14; Heb. 5–7), the lamb (Ex. 12; John 1:29), and the brazen serpent (Num. 21:8-9; John 3:14). The Jewish sacrificial system is a type of the sacrifice of Christ (Heb. 10:1-18), as are the rituals and furnishings of the tabernacle and temple (Heb. 8).

4. Jesus wasn't speaking about the Communion (Lord's Supper, Eucharist) when He spoke about eating His flesh

and drinking His blood. He hadn't even instituted the Lord's Supper for His disciples, so why would He discuss it with a congregation of rebellious unconverted Jews? He was using metaphorical language to explain spiritual truth, and the people took it literally, as they often did (John 2:19-21; 3:4; 4:11, 32; 8:30-36; 11:11-13).

5. Paul used the gathering of the manna as an illustration of Christian giving (2 Cor. 8:13-15). Each person in the Corinthian church would bring what God had directed them to give; and when it was all put together, it met the needs.

**Chapter 7**

1. David's men thought of stoning him when they all came home and found their families and possessions gone (1 Sam. 30:1-6). How this would have solved the problem is a mystery. The Jewish people wanted to stone Jesus (John 8:59; 10:31), and they actually did stone Stephen (Acts 7:58).

2. This miracle must not be confused with a similar one described in Numbers 20:1-13, even though the name "Meribah" is used in both accounts (Ex. 17:7; Num. 20:13). The Israelites caused contention on more than one occasion!

3. The rabbis had a tradition that the rock that Moses smote accompanied the Jews throughout their wilderness journey and provided water, but there's no biblical basis for this. In 1 Corinthians 10:4, Paul said that it was the spiritual rock that accompanied them, not a literal rock, and that Christ was that *spiritual* Rock.

4. The Book of Hebrews uses the experiences of the people of Israel to illustrate the important spiritual truth that it is by faith that we enter into our inheritance and enjoy what God has planned for us. At Kadesh-Barnea, Israel refused to obey God and enter the land, so they stayed in the wilderness for thirty-eight more years until that unbelieving older generation died. It's because of unbelief that God's people

today miss God's best for their lives. Our task is to hear His voice (the Word), believe what He says, and obey His will. He will take care of the rest.

5. For an exposition of the Book of Joshua, see my book *Be Strong,* published by Chariot Victor.

6. This is probably not the Hur whose son constructed the tabernacle (31:2; 35:30; 38:22; 1 Chron. 2:19-20). See Exodus 24:14. Jewish tradition says he was married to Miriam and therefore was brother-in-law to Moses and Aaron, but there's no biblical evidence for this.

7. The Greek verb gives us our English word "agonize" and was applied to athletes striving for victory (1 Cor. 9:25) and soldiers fighting a battle (1 Tim. 6:12). The NIV translates it "wrestling in prayer for you."

8. The NIV margin reads "Because a hand was against the throne of the Lord," referring to the attack of the Amalekites. The ASV margin agrees, "Because there is a hand against the throne of Jehovah." This would explain why God declared perpetual war on the Amalekites, for they had arrogantly attacked the God of Israel. The NRSVB translates the phrase "a hand upon the banner," suggesting that the Jews "lay hold of God" by faith whenever they find themselves attacked. Banners were used to rally the troops (Isa. 13:2), declare war (31:9), alert the army (Jer. 51:12, 27), and declare victory (Ex. 17:15).

9. See 24:4, 7; 34:27; Num. 33:1-2; Deut. 25:17-19; 31:9, 24.

10. We have met Gershom ("stranger, alien") in 2:22, but 18:4 is the first time the younger son Eliezer ("my God is my help") is mentioned in the Bible. Like the names Joseph gave to his two sons (Gen. 41:50-52), the names of Moses' sons reflected his own experience: an alien in the land, but with God's help, a conqueror.

11. Numbers 31:14, 28 indicate that the army was organized on a similar plan. See 1 Samuel 22:7; 1 Chronicles 12.

12. Since Israel was a strong patriarchal society, the emphasis is on men, but throughout Scripture, the Lord called and used many gifted women to serve Him and His people.

## Chapter 8

1. The biblical record from Exodus 19:1 through Numbers 10:10 tells what happened in the camp during the eleven months the Jews were at Sinai. Moses received the Law and shared it with the people; the workers constructed the tabernacle and its furnishings; the priesthood was established and instructed; and the people were numbered and the tribes organized for their march to Kadesh-Barnea.

2. See Exodus 5:1; 7:16; 8:1, 20; 9:1, 13; 10:3, 26.

3. It seems that eight times Moses went up the mountain and met with God and then descended to speak to the people. Some of the ascents and descents are implied because you find Moses addressing either God or the nation.

| Ascended | Descended |
|---|---|
| 19:3 | 19:7 (implied) |
| 19:8 | 19:14 |
| 19:20 | 19:25 |
| 20:21 | 24:1-3 (implied) |
| 24:9, 13, 15, 18 | 32:15 |
| 32:31 | 33:4 (inferred) |
| 33:12 (inferred) | 34:1-3 (inferred) |
| 34:4 | 34:29 |

4. The eagle is identified with Israel not only in the matter of their deliverance from Egypt (Ex. 19:4) and their maturity (Deut. 32:11-12), but also with reference to their release from Babylonian Captivity (Isa. 40:31) and their future safety during the time of Jacob's trouble described in Revelation 6–19 (12:13-14).

5. Some students believe that the Parable of the Treasure (Matt. 13:44) refers especially to Israel, God's treasure. On the cross, Jesus purchased the field ("the world," 13:38) and "hid" Israel in it until that time when the promises will be fulfilled and the nation will enter the Messianic Kingdom.

6. The admonition for the men not to have intercourse with their wives (v. 15) does not in any way imply that the act is defiling. Later, when Moses expounded the Law, he would deal with this matter (Lev. 15:16-18).

7. The section from Exodus 20:22–23:33 is known as "The Book of the Covenant" and was ratified through sacrifices by Moses and the people (24:1-8; Heb. 9:18-22). "The Book of the Covenant" was an expansion and application of some of the Ten Commandments to the life of the Jewish people.

8. Jesus didn't point the rich young ruler to the Law to tell him how to be saved, but to convince him that he needed to be saved (Mark 10:17-31). The only person who perfectly kept the Law was Jesus Christ, and He did it for us.

9. The Law is a yoke that burdens us (Gal. 5:1; Acts 15:10), but the yoke of Christ gives us rest (Matt. 11:28-30). The Law is a debt that we can't pay, so Christ paid it for us (Luke 7:36-50; Col. 2:14). Living under Law means living in the shadows (Col. 2:16-17; Heb. 8:4-5; 10:1), but trusting Christ means living in the light of reality (John 8:12; 1 John 1:5-10).

10. For the origin of polytheism and idolatry, read Romans 1:18-32.

11. The prohibition against making idols doesn't interfere with mankind's right to artistic creative expression. The Jews were commanded to make a beautiful tabernacle and later a beautiful temple, and in both of them there were objects patterned after things in God's creation. To create artistic things is one matter; to worship them is quite something else.

12. The promise in verse 12 is initially for the nation, assuring the Jews that obedience would keep them in their land a long time, but in Ephesians 6:1-3 Paul applied it to individual believers.

13. We have barely scratched the surface in our study of this important portion of Scripture. For further study, see: *The Ten Commandments*, by R.W. Dale (Hodder and Stoughton, 1910); *The Ten Commandments for Today,* by William Barclay (Harper & Row, 1973); *Playing by the Rules,* by D. Stuart Briscoe (Revell, 1986); *Lifelines: The Ten Commandments for Today*, by Edith Schaeffer (Crossway, 1982); *Foundations for Reconstruction,* by Elton Trueblood (Word paperback edition, 1972); *The Ten Commandments,* by Thomas Watson (Banner of Truth, 1965); and *The Eleven Commandments,* by Lehman Strauss (Loizeaux, 1955).

## Chapter 9

1. See John 1:18; 5:37; 6:46; Colossians 1:15; 1 Timothy 1:17; 6:16; Hebrews 11:27.

2. Jacques Ellul, *The Humiliation of the Word* (Grand Rapids: William B. Eerdmans, 1985), 86. The entire chapter ("Idols and the Word") is an insightful discussion of the dangers involved in replacing hearing the Word with trying to "see" something remarkable from God or about God. God is incomprehensible and "wholly other," and we can't begin to understand His nature or His will apart from what He chooses to say to us. An idol is not only a substitute for the person of God but also for the Word of God.

3. Abraham Joshua Heschel, *I Asked for Wonder: A Spiritual Anthology,* Samuel H. Dresner, editor (New York: Crossroad, 1996), 73. It's unfortunate that, in Jesus' day, some of the scribes and Pharisees had made an idol of the Scriptures and failed to know the God of the Scriptures (John 5:37-47).

4. Well-to-do men sometimes had concubines who were looked upon as legal but "secondary" wives. The law protected them from being classified as ordinary slaves and saw to it they were given their rights (Deut. 21:10-14).

5. The Latin word *talis* means "such like" and gives us the English word "retaliate," which means "to pay back in kind." The *lex talionis* (law of retaliation) was a principle that kept people from taking revenge and requiring more punishment than the crime demanded, as it were, killing a mosquito with a cannon.

6. As far as the criminal courts are concerned, the goal is to free the innocent and condemn the guilty, but when it comes to our relationship to God, *there are no innocent people.* "All have sinned and come short of the glory of God" (Rom. 3:23). But in His grace, because of Christ's sacrifice on the cross, God can declare righteous any guilty sinner who believes on Jesus Christ (4:5). God justifies the wicked and so changes them that they don't live wicked lives anymore!

7. Because of this law, orthodox Jews will not have milk and meat together at a meal.

## Chapter 10

1. God is both transcendent and immanent, high above us and close to us, and we must maintain a balanced outlook in our theology and our worship. If we overemphasize the transcendent, we may try to worship a God so far away that He's beyond helping us, but if we stress only the immanent, we may try to be so unduly familiar with God that we fail to honor His greatness. The secret is balance.

2. The Old Testament tabernacle had many different names, including: the tent of meeting (27:21), the tabernacle of the Lord (Lev. 17:4), the tent/tabernacle of testimony (Num. 1:50; 9:15), the sanctuary of the Lord (19:20), the

house of God (Jud. 18:31), the house of the Lord (1 Sam. 1:7), and the temple of the Lord (v. 9).

3. When the Jews entered the Promised Land, the ark was first located in Gilgal (Josh. 4:19; 9:6), but then Shiloh became its home (9:27; 18:1; 19:51; 22:12; Jud. 21:12; 1 Sam. 4–5). The Philistines returned the ark to Kiriath-Jearim where it stayed for twenty years (6:21–7:2). After David's aborted attempt to bring the ark to Jerusalem, it was placed in the house of Obed-Edom for three months (2 Sam. 6:1-11) and then was brought to Jerusalem (vv. 12-19). David's great desire was to build a beautiful house for the ark, but God chose his son Solomon instead (2 Sam. 7; 1 Chron. 17). The last time we meet the ark in Scripture is in the heavenly temple (Rev. 11:19). In that context, it is a symbol of the faithfulness of God to keep His covenant with His people, and an assurance that His law will be vindicated and His glory revealed.

4. The Hebrew text doesn't have the word "ephah" in verse 5, so we really don't know how much flour was used for each loaf. If the measure was indeed an ephah, then each loaf was made from about four quarts of flour—and that's a large loaf! Could two rows of six loaves that large fit on such a small table? Or were the six loaves stacked on top of each other?

5. The Hebrew text of Exodus 27:20 reads "that they may be kept burning continually."

## Chapter 11

1. These are not prayers offered by people in heaven who have been "made saints" and through whom people on earth can pray. All who have trusted Jesus Christ as Lord and Savior are saints (set-apart ones) and have the privilege of prayer. The two passages in the Book of Revelation teach us that no true prayer of faith offered by God's children is ever

lost but will be answered in God's way and God's time.

2. What is traditionally called the "Lord's Prayer" should be called the "Disciple's Prayer," because our Lord could never pray it. He never said "Our Father" in His prayers, and He certainly didn't need to ask for the forgiveness of sin! This prayer can be prayed meaningfully, from the heart, but it must not be recited carelessly like a religious charm. Basically, this prayer gives us a pattern to follow: God's concerns come first (vv. 9-10) before we bring our own requests (vv. 11-13). Our own personal requests must be tested by whether or not we're sincerely concerned about honoring God's name, hastening God's kingdom, and doing God's will. Prayer isn't getting our will done in heaven; it's getting God's will done on earth.

3. All of our speech is to be "seasoned with salt" (Col. 4:6), which suggests that we ought to speak to people with the same holy reverence that we speak to God, for He hears what we say. The ability we have to speak to each other is as much a sacred gift of God as the privilege of prayer. Note how David connects the two in Psalm 141:1-3.

4. For an exposition of the meaning of the sacrifices listed in Leviticus 1–7, see my book *Be Holy* (Chariot Victor).

5. In washing their feet, our Lord also taught the disciples the importance of humble service to one another. They occasionally wanted to seek the highest places, but Jesus gave them an example of taking the lowest place.

6. Blue, purple, and scarlet are found together twenty-four times in the Book of Exodus. The priestly garments include gold, blue, and purple (28:6, 15; 39:2, 5, 8).

## Chapter 12

1. The doctrine of "the priesthood of believers" is a precious one, for it means that each believer has the privilege of entering into God's presence to worship, pray, and seek

NOTES

God's will. Note that Peter speaks of the priesthood *collectively* ("a holy priesthood . . . a royal priesthood, a holy nation") even though he writes to believers in five different provinces (1 Peter 1:1). It's dangerous for a believer to separate himself or herself from the rest of God's people and hope to learn the will of God. We belong to each other and we need each other. Isolated priests can become troublemakers in the church.

2. The Jewish priesthood belonged to the order of Aaron, while the priesthood of Christ belongs to the order of Melchizedek (Heb. 5:1-10; 7:1–8:13). Melchizedek was both a king and a priest (Gen. 14:18-24; Ps. 110:4), while Aaron was only a priest. When King Uzziah tried to force himself into the priesthood, God smote him with leprosy (2 Chron. 26:16-23), for the two offices of king and priest weren't united until the priestly ministry of Christ. The Aaronic priests never finished their work, because the blood of bulls and goats couldn't take away sin, but Christ finished the work of redemption by shedding His own blood. The tabernacle had no chairs for the priests to rest, but Jesus has sat down on the throne in heaven because He finished His work. The Old Testament high priests died and had to be replaced, but Jesus lives forever by the power of an endless life (Heb. 7:16). See my book *Be Confident* for an exposition of Hebrews 6–10.

3. The jewels on the high priest's shoulders and on the breastplate remind us that our High Priest in heaven carries us on His shoulders and over His heart. He is touched with the feelings of our infirmities and gives us the grace we need when we come to His throne and ask (Heb. 2:17-18; 4:14-16; 7:25-28).

4. It is sometimes said that on the Day of Atonement, the bells indicated to the people outside that the high priest was still alive and God had accepted the sacrifices. But the high

209

priest didn't wear his beautiful robes on the Day of Atonement, but only simple linen garments of humiliation (Lev. 16:4), so there were no bells tinkling in the tabernacle. He didn't put on his official robes until after the scapegoat had been released and the high priest had washed himself (Lev. 16:23-24).

## Chapter 13

1. Phillips Brooks, *The Influence of Jesus* (London: H.R. Allenson), 191.

2. Some have defended Aaron by saying that the golden calf was supposed to represent God (v. 4) and not replace Him, but their arguments are weak. It was unlawful for a Jew to make any representation of Jehovah, and Aaron knew it. Unable to control the people, he compromised with them and encouraged their sin.

3. The phrase "rose up to play" in 32:6 is described in verses 18-19. Their feast was a demonstration of idol worship with all its sensuality and immorality. The word "naked" in verse 25 can also mean "to cast off restraint." Aaron allowed the people to do whatever they wanted to do, and their evil hearts took over.

4. At least three times in his career, Moses put the people of God ahead of his own interests. In Egypt, he gave up his future as a royal prince to identify with the people of God in their trials (Heb. 11:24-26). On Mt. Sinai, he refused God's offer to make a new nation out of him and his descendants (Ex. 32:10), and he refused the same offer a second time at Kadesh-Barnea (Num. 14:1-20). Moses made his mistakes, but by every measure you can find, he was a great man and a great leader.

5. In Scripture, committing sin is sometimes compared to eating and drinking. See Job 15:16; 20:12-19; Ps. 109:18; Prov. 4:17; 9:17; 18:8; 20:17; 26:22.

# NOTES

6. The "Book of Life" is the book in which the names of the living are recorded and then blotted out when they die. See Psalms 9:5; 69:28. It must not be confused with the Lamb's Book of Life which records the names of the saved (Rev. 13:8; 17:8; 20:15; 21:27). An unforgiven sinner was in danger of being killed by the Lord (2 Sam. 12:13). Paul was willing to be eternally condemned for the sake of the Jews (Rom. 9:3), and Jesus did die and suffer judgment for the sake of His people as well as the whole world (Isa. 53:4-6, 8).

7. Truly spiritual people don't recognize their own godliness but usually feel as though they're failures and far from what they ought to be. At Pentecost (Acts 2), each believer could see the tongues of fire above the other believers' heads, but not over their own heads.

8. The Greek word for "transformed" in 2 Corinthians 3:18 is "transfigured," as in Matthew 17:2. It describes the glory on the inside being revealed on the outside. Moses only *reflected* the glory of God; the dedicated believer *radiates* the glory of God. Unlike Moses, we don't wear a veil when we come to God's Word because we have nothing to hide.

9. The statement in verse 33 "So Moses finished the work" reminds us of Christ's prayer in John 17:4 and His cry from the cross, "It is finished" (John 19:30), as well as Paul's words, "I have finished my course, I have kept the faith" (2 Tim. 4:7). How important it is in the Christian life to end well.

# Titles already available in the Old Testament "Be Series"

*Be Amazed (Hosea, Joel, Jonah, Nahum, Habbakuk, Malachi)
*Be Authentic (Genesis 25-50)
 Be Available (Judges)
*Be Basic (Genesis 1-11)
 Be Comforted (Isaiah)
 Be Committed (Ruth, Esther)
*Be Concerned (Amos, Obadiah, Micah, Zephaniah)
 Be Decisive (Jeremiah)
 Be Determined (Nehemiah)
*Be Heroic (Haggai, Zechariah, Ezra)
 Be Holy (Leviticus)
 Be Obedient (Life of Abraham/Genesis 12-24)
 Be Patient (Job)
 Be Satisfied (Ecclesiastes)
 Be Skillful (Proverbs)
 Be Strong (Joshua)

*Personal and Group Study Guide Included

# If you liked this book, check out these great titles from Chariot Victor Publishing . . .

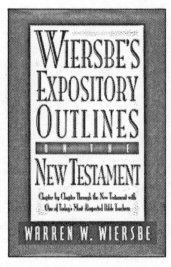
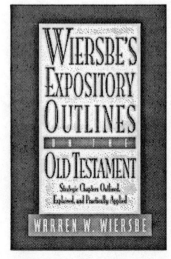